AT ALL TIMES
&
IN ALL PLACES

AT ALL TIMES
&
IN ALL PLACES

The prayer and worship handbook

Myra Blyth & Tony Jasper

Marshall Pickering

Marshall Morgan and Scott
Marshall Pickering
3 Beggarwood Lane, Basingstoke, Hants RG23 7LP, UK

First published in 1986
by Marshall Morgan and Scott Publications Ltd
Part of the Marshall Pickering Holdings Group
A subsidiary of the Zondervan Corporation

ISBN: 0 551 01333 8

Text set in Plantin
by Brian Robinson, Ball Moor, Buckingham

Printed in Great Britain
by Hazell Watson & Viney Ltd, Aylesbury Bucks.

CONTENTS

For the Sunday At Eight group, Chapel Street Methodist Church, Penzance. Sylvia Gordon, Jean Brotherton and Margaret Lister, whose faith lives and thrives in spite of . . . who have taught me a great deal.

Tony Jasper

For Robert Blyth

Myra Blyth

Acknowledgements

Material by Conrad Weiser is from *Dancing All The Dances Singing All the Songs.* Copyright © 1975 by Fortress Press, Philadelphia, USA. 'Call to Worship' and 'For All People' from *No Longer Strangers* edited by Iben Gjerding and Katherine Kinnamon, WCC publications, Geneva, 1984. 'The World' by Bethel AZ Kiplagat is from *Risk* Vol 9. No. 3. WCC, Geneva. Psalm 129 is from Leslie F. Brandt. *Modern Reading of the Psalms—Psalms Now,* Concordia, USA. 'Here Am I' by Steve Turner from *Up To Date,* Hodder and Stoughton. 'The Dream' by Martin Luther King is from *My Life With Martin Luther King, Jr.,* Hodder and Stoughton. 'Commitment: Community Worship' from *Worship And Live,* Eucharist Congregation of Ashram Community, Sheffield. 'He Lives' from *Discovery In Prayer,* Sister Athena, Paulist Press. 'Litany' and 'God of Abraham', from *Your Word Is Near,* Huub Oosterhuis.

Poems by Stewart Henderson, copyright S. Henderson. 'Loveislightlifewarm', copyright Mrs Alex Mitchell. 'Don't Dance On The Wire', copyright Vince Cross, 1983. 'New People, New Paths', and 'We Live In Hope' by Richard D. Orr, by permission of Judson Press, Valley Forge, USA. 'There is Dignity Here', from The Song of the Magi, *Now* magazine of the Overseas Division of the Methodist Church, originally from *Suffering* and *Hope*, permission of the Christian Conference of Asia.

'Christmas for Others', Tony Jasper is from *Thank God,* Lion Publishing. 'Sharon's Christmas Prayer' is from *The Hour of the Unexpected,* John Shea, reprinted by permission of Argus Communications, USA. 'Why Travel So Far', permission from Overseas Division of the Methodist Church, Britain and formerly printed in *Now.* 'How Can I

What is worship?

Editors Iben Gjerding and Katherine Kinnamon, in their excellent resource book for women and worship, *No Longer Strangers*, have these words to say about worship:

Through song, prayer, proclamation, confession and forgiveness, the sequence of the service assists the participants:

* to recall and reflect on the savings acts of God recorded in scripture;
* to find and celebrate the presence of God in everyday life;
* to lay before God their deepest fears, joys and hopes;
* to dare to acknowledge the holy within their lives and within the ordinary things of daily experience;
* to find hope through the goodness of God within their personal and communal lives;
* to give thanks for God's gracious love, expressed through Jesus Christ.

For modern-day Christians living in urban and suburban environments, surrounded by the complexity of the modern world, seeing God is obscured. We go through the rituals of His church. We are more or less mindful of His commandments. We may or may not feel His presence in our lives, giving us comfort and direction, but how often do we see and hear Him speaking in our services of worship? How often is His presence revealed in our liturgy?

His presence is symbolised in myriad ways in His holy temple, but these symbols, through time, veil rather than reveal His presence. They lose their shine. They become ritualised, mechanised, unseen by the wondering eye of the child within us. 'Except you become as a little child, you shall not enter the kingdom of heaven.' What is this 'becoming as a little child'?

Part of 'becoming as a child' is being able to attend to an experience before naming it, to wonder without words. As we gain in cerebral exercise and in analytical understanding we often lose the richness of our immediate sensing. We must seek to look with new eyes at the elements of our worship that we might see our God through His symbols—incense, candle, cross, priest, and through the experiences of song and prayer, ancient voices new in our hearing. Then our manufactured, plastic world, our world of economic forces, great powers and the kingship of things will recede, and we will hear again the still, small voice and see in the circle of smoke and the flame of a candle the face of the Lord our God[1].

Praise the Lord, O my soul
And all that is within me, bless his holy name.

How to use this book

Learning from each other

Many people are gifted in writing and their skill can reveal things to us that we had not dreamed of or expected. That is one reason why worship compilations can prove useful. However they should not be seen as collections that save us the time and effort we need to put into our own preparations for worship.

Once a particular prayer or poem has been chosen, the way it is read is of critical importance, whether by a group

---

1. Taken from the introduction to the worship services of St Stephen and the Incarnation.

or an individual. Words can become meaningless if they are spoken without understanding. I suspect we have all suffered at the hands of someone experimenting with a new form of worship and doing it rather badly. We rarely say anything but resolve not to come next time that particular individual is leading the gathering. It is important that we find loving ways to share our responses with one another so we can move forward together. Perhaps you may have an idea that particular reading could have been enhanced? Get involved. Find a way to offer your suggestion. Remember though, that people venturing into new areas are usually insecure and sensitive to criticism. Make a positive comment before offering your suggestion for improvement. With sensitivity much can be achieved.

Preparing for worship

Remember no room is the same. Acoustics differ from place to place. A slow, dragging song can be infused with life and vitality if the tempo is changed slightly. Remember too that gatherings differ so, where possible, become aware of the make-up of the group beforehand. As a worship leader you are called to be yourself, not some kind of religious person with affected voice and mannerisms. You are not elevating yourself but the words used, you are bringing people closer to God and to themselves and you are interpreting gospel truths.

Working with a group

In some situations it is not easy to delegate and you will be leading worship on your own. In other situations delegation works quite well and you may find yourself working with a group of people. Try and explore the talents of the group, observing general speaking habits and character traits. Some people are naturally exuberant, others more withdrawn and reflective. These moods may be useful in choosing someone to reflect particular thoughts. Of course the small group extrovert can become uncontrollably shy when placed in an unknown context and deprived of the capacity to self-exhibit!

A sensitive worship leader should be tuned-in to all the group and to how each individual can participate. Sometimes there can be surprises as people flourish because of the trust placed in them. Obviously some people are better with words than others. They can more naturally interpret and project and may even have some form of drama, voice or theatrical experience. That said, it does not mean that they should necessarily dominate. Encourage them to build up those who appear less talented. Within the group there will be some more adept at singing, others at dance or mime. Group organisers should be on the look-out for hidden talent. Many people are unaware of their gifts and need encouragement to draw them out.

Try not to just 'throw things at people' and expect them to function. Give them a chance to read their material through beforehand. It is important to show them how their material relates to the overall context of the service. In this way you avoid having a series of spoken units that bear little relation to each other or to the rest of the service.

Making yourself heard

Practise reading your material aloud before the service. Have someone listen to you from the furthest points in the building to see if you can be heard. Even without microphones several factors can enhance audibility. Projecting your voice is important. Practise 'throwing your voice' to the back wall of the room as loudly as possible and then gradually decrease it until it feels comfortable and is pleasant to listen to. Pronounce your words clearly as this will make you much more easily heard. Large buildings often have a time lag or echo. Again, practise speaking until you find a pace that feels comfortable to you. It will be slower than normal speech but should not sound stilted.

12

Basics

Remember the basic preparations for any worship gathering: lots of prayer, a spiritual and cultural awareness, relevant biblical emphasis, and the creation of a positive atmosphere. A growing number of churches are breathing light and colour, giving space and freedom and encouraging the visual. The days of thirty minute sermons as the main part of the service are past. At certain times and occasions and with a particularly gifted preacher this may be appropriate. However on many occasions the sermon can be a place for exciting experimentation. Encourage movement, an address spoken from the aisles or front pews, experiment with speaker/congregation participation. Services can be quite relaxed and make use of music, art, dance and drama. Pay attention to decor. It takes skill and sensitivity to fit the ethos of an old-style building with the demands of the present. Thought must equally be given to what are sometimes regarded as 'standard' fittings: an established organist and choir. Tact and humour can often produce positive results and make room for experimentation. Try not to regard the organist and choir as a nuisance because you may want to run a tape of a gospel choir. Everyone has talents to offer.

How to use this book

The material in this book is divided into eight sections. Where it seemed helpful to give some words of explanation on how to use particular readings, directions have been given at the beginning of the relevant section.

PART ONE

Words of Adoration

He Lives! He Lives!
So many ways to meet Him
God keeps pushing things along
God affects everything
To know Him!
Jesus—the Bread of Life
Where things happen—you meet Him!
Loveislightlifewarm
Holy God

Notes on Part One extracts

He lives! He lives! Use one voice for the cry 'He Lives!' and a different voice for the rest of the poem. If the gathering have copies they can shout out with joy those two words. The imagery asks for visual accompaniment. If you want to use music try the pulsating rhythms of the opening or instrumental Break of the Big Money from Rush (Vertigo VERH 31: this title is also available as a single).

So many ways to meet Him. The last stanza can be said by all.

God keeps pushing things along. This can be said in procession around the church, the gathering stopping at various places at which important moments in the lives of the biblical characters mentioned would be portrayed visually. Alternatively, visual images could be displayed at the front of the building to be shown at the appropriate time. The reading can be done in two parts. One reader begins with the 'God of' narratives and then everyone joins in with the words 'We anticipate what is not yet'. All voices continue on from there until the end of the reading.

God affects everything. This can be accompanied by visual imagery or dance.

To know Him. This should be said with some degree of reverence and might be prefaced with the words, 'A prayer for all of us'.

Jesus—the Bread of Life. Visual images could be used to accompany this reading.

Loveislightlifewarm. This is written for some kind of visual interpretation, dance, mime or something more static.

Holy God. This can be read by one voice throughout or divided between several voices.

He lives! He lives!
Always and forever: the Lord!

The rocks cry out
and part in wonder
Sun beams
and throws out its arms
awakening the world
to glorious truth
He lives!
Wind plays with petals
teasing, caressing
in mood so delightful
stirring the flowers
and grasses
and scurrying insects
to nature's own rhythm
He lives!
Then man
who is master
of wind, rock and nature
joins heart, mind and voice
to earth's ringing gladness
His whole being looks out
and inward too
for new life
God's life
is quickening anew—
He lives!

Sister Athena

So many ways to meet Him

God, our Father,
by living we learn what creation means—
   that, out of love, you fashioned us, human,
   weak, so that we need each other and you,
   yet strong enough to say Yes when you call.
We thank you for this creation, Father,
   that in all the works of your hands,
   we find traces of love;
   that in life's beauty we discover you,
   and in life's pain we grow to maturity as your children.

What we have learned with our ears
   and seen with our eyes
   in the life of Jesus Christ,
   may we now proclaim to all the world:
   that we are the sons and daughters of the living God
   created in love,
   and destined for life.

All glory be to you Father,
   through your Son, Jesus Christ,
   with the Spirit who brings life and blessing
   forever and ever.

Amen

John R. Hogan, SJ

God keeps pushing things along

God of Abraham
night and desert
star in the heaven
name in his flesh
seed in the dead
womb of his wife.
God of Jacob
wrestling stranger
fists that struck him
wound in his thigh.
God of Moses
burning voice, fire
under his feel
world like a cloud
pillar before him
water and bread
land of the promise
God of David
harp in his hands
song in his mouth
love surpassing
the love of women
his house's foundation
child of his sin
cold in his bones,
God in Babel
God unspeakable
scattered abroad
God of the dead.
God of Job
man of sorrows
humiliated
lacking all form
dust a twig

weighed in the scales
of the world.

God of Jesus
shadow over
a Jewish girl
God of Auschwitz
you have blown
the ashes of Jews
over my feet.
God of me
tongue of snow
and of rapture
voice that catches
in my throat
storm head-wind
covering me
tender rigid
like a body.
God of no one
simply people
march of ages
stranger we come
slowly to know
you elusive
stone of the sages
you not God
as we think you
furnace of silence
difficult friend.

We anticipate
what is not yet
and practise now
your future
we say and sing
that all you have made
your creation is good

laboriously
so very slowly
we work out your promise
in hope and fear
and strive to build
a city of peace
a new creation
where you will be
our light, our all.

Give us strength, O God,
to persevere
and bring us to
a happy end.

Huub Oosterhuis

God affects everything

A prayer of adoration

O wind in our Faces, Fire in our souls, Joy in our midst,
Thunder upon many waters;
Majesty surrounding us, Steadfastness supporting us,
Graciousness beckoning us, Love welcoming us:
Now is the daylight upon us and our hearts full
    of expectancy as your promises advance upon us.
The cities stir from slumber, the country wakens
    from sleep, the villages arise for a new day;
all that comes to be alive with your life,
and that life is the light of men.
Blessed are you, our God, for ever and ever.

Rev Dr E. S. P. Jones

To know Him!

I pray to you, my God,
and call you by your name,
but cannot lay hold of you
because you are greater than a name
and smaller than a word,
more silent than all silence in the world.
Make me receptive to you,
give me a living heart
and new eyes
to see you, hidden and invisible,
to take you as you are
when you come without power,
and, in my weakness, in my death,
to know who you are.

Amen

Jesus—the Bread of Life

Jesus has said very clearly:
  I am the love to be loved
  I am the life to be lived
  I am the joy to be shared
  I am the bread to be eaten
  I am the blood to be drunk
  I am the truth to be told
  I am the light to be lit
  I am the peace to be given.
Jesus is everything.

Mother Teresa

Where things happen—you meet Him!

'We respond to this Christ, who became our brother, as a family. We speak to him in our own language and he answers us; we welcome him with all that is best in our cultural heritage, our art, our music, our dances, our ornaments, our stored wisdom. We respond to Christ as a family; in other words, as a human community and as a cosmic community. In our confession of faith, in our worship, in the humble confession of our sins, and in our joy in the salvation held out to us in Christ, we bring, as it were, an offering in praise of God, not only with the voice of the human community but also with the voice of the cosmos.'

Engelbert Mveng

Loveislightlifewarm

Loveislightlifewarm
God's love,
Reality.
Darklifts, gloomdawns,
Lightrises
Sun.

SunGod,
Jesus,
Lifelove, dearheart,
Lightlinger, touchsoft,
Sweet
Love.

Alex Beale
(Now Mrs Alex Mitchell)

Holy God

Holy God,
we have come to worship you and praise your name, in song and deed. We confess, however, God; that it is easier to call you father, than it is Lord, for we frequently would like to have our own way rather than yours. We are glad that you know us each and every Sunday that we come, but clearly we would like to hide from you on many of the other times in our life. God, father, the one who sees into all the moments of our existence, thank you for never going away, even when we want you to and thank you for your great love that sent us Jesus Christ, our Lord and Saviour, in whose name we pray, Amen.

PART TWO

Words for Our Time

Notes on Part Two extracts

Different times and situations have seen people translating historic creeds and beliefs into words that relate to their specific and known situations. Tell of this process or ask the gathering: 'How do we make sense of our gospel in modern terms, in language that firmly reminds people that God has come to us?' Then suggest one of the following affirmations, or form groups that might in some way compose their own. Much of the material in this section is a response to the social and political upheavals of our time. If a number of these extracts are used together set them within a larger context in which the gathering has been encouraged to consider the global implications of the gospel as it relates to the social and political circumstances of our particular time. Take the opportunity to listen to the experience of Christians from many different cultures and countries.

Affirmation. This can be said by all, standing, at a fairly good pace or it can be divided between two voices, reading alternately. For example, Reader 1 begins, 'With gratitude . . . and risen Lord.' Then Reader 2 says, 'We know . . . Lord of all.'

Wanted—real Christians. This can employ different voices and each section might be read by people who can offer various jobs and roles within the Christian community.

For all people. This can use a number of voices. A musical illustration of chaos can precede it, e.g. the track Revolution 9 on the Beatles white album.

His dying and rising—for us! This is ideally suited to mime gestures.

My people, I am your security. This is long and does not seem suitable for reading in a service although occasionally a long reading can be indulged in. It helps to distribute copies beforehand for people to follow. Certainly good, clear readers are necessary for it not to be unwieldy.

29

Lord, guide me. Before reading this why not ask people to tell of their feelings in translating the gospel into concrete situations; of their responses to God's call on their lives at different times. See this also in great biblical figures like Jeremiah and in Christians whose lives have been the subject of biography and autobiography.

The other Britain is long and can benefit from people being aware of its main points beforehand. Vary the voices, perhaps placing readers behind a table to represent a reporting team or media ensemble!

Prisoners of conscience serves as a good introduction before meeting with or hearing from those people familiar with the stifling of their personal freedom.

His way in confrontation and disputes comes from an editorial in a religious newspaper. Why not suggest that people offer short 'editorials' on the events of the day from a Christian/biblical perspective?

Greater love hath no man than this says something about humanity, and about what happens when the worst is faced. It captures grief and yet hope. That hope is in the cross and resurrection of our Lord. Use one voice for the narrator and other voices for the various speakers quoted. Sing some seafaring hymns like Brightly Beams Our Father's Mercy, Eternal Father Strong To Save, etc. Perhaps some of the gathering know of other re-writes of the 23rd Psalm similar to the Fisherman's Psalm.

Enjoying a lifestyle. Charts, diagrams, maps, relevant posters from organisations involved in the struggle to live justly might decorate the foyer and form the basis of prayer stemming from these thoughts.

It's all bigger than our small world might preface a call to commitment. Certainly it would lift such a call out of a self-centred context and replace it with a much broader vision.

Affirmation

With gratitude and joy we affirm again
our confidence in the sufficiency of our crucified
and risen Lord.

We know him as the one who is, and who was, and
who is to come,
the sovereign Lord of all.

To the individual he comes with power
to liberate him from every evil and sin,
from every power in heaven and earth,
and from every threat of life or death.

To the world he comes as the Lord of the universe:
with deep compassion for the poor and the hungry,
to liberate the powerless and the oppressed;
to the powerful and the oppressors he comes
in judgement and mercy.

We see God at work today
both within the church and beyond the church
towards the achievement of his purpose
that justice might shine on every nation.

He calls his church to be part of his saving activity
both in calling men and women to decisive personal
response
to his Lordship,
and in unequivocal commitment to the movements and
works
by which all may know justice
and have opportunity to be fully human.

In joyous trust in Christ's power and victory
we can live with freedom and hope
whatever the present may be.

The Lord is at hand.

Pauline Webb

Creed for a nuclear age

We believe in Jesus Christ,
Crucified, risen and ascended,
Who has battled with evil and won,
He has won with the power of his Love,
Love which is stronger than all the evil and violence in
the world.
We believe in the power of his Love,
Power alive in his people today,
Power to overcome fear and suspicion.
And we put our trust in his Love alone,
And we turn away from all nuclear weapons,
That kill our innocent brothers and sisters,
For we cannot rely on the weapons of this world
When all our security, hope, and life is in Jesus.
We believe in the power of the risen Christ,
For only he can give us inward security.
And we turn away from the evil of mass destruction,
Of arming ourselves while others starve,
Of trusting the weapons of evil
To safeguard the true and the good.
We believe in Jesus Christ;
And we trust his power of Love and nothing else.

*Used at Mannafest, outside Lincoln Cathedral and during a
vigil outside RAF Scampton (Vulcan base).*

Wanted . . . real Christians

Wanted. Young men and women for challenging and demanding positions. There are urgent vacancies for young people who are offered the prospect of real life. Candidates should be able to bear mocking and scoffing. Have the courage of their convictions, and be able to stand at all times for what they know to be right. The support of unlimited resources is available to all who will accept the position of being real Christians.

Wanted. Workers. God is at work in the world and is urgently seeking partners. Those who are prepared to work with God should offer their services immediately to him. Only the totally unqualified need apply. As this is a family concern all applicants will not only be given the duties of servants but the privileges of Sonship.

Wanted. People to pray. Must be prepared to pray regularly and faithfully. These are key appointments on which the worldwide success of the work depends. These vacancies are open to all, irrespective of age or sex. The rewards are great. There are unlimited vacancies for this job.

Wanted. People who are prepared to love their neighbours. This demanding job is offered to all. This responsible position requires of those applying that first they must be prepared to love God with all their heart, soul and mind.

Wanted. To feed the hungry, to welcome the stranger, to clothe the naked, to visit the sick, to care for the prisoners. Vacancies exist for all the above positions.

Wanted. The tired. The weary. The frustrated. The fearful. The defeated. The weak. The heavily laden. Total security is offered. No superannuation or insurance is offered as it is not intended that those appointed should die.

Only sinners need apply.
All applicants will be successful.

Wanted. Disciples to follow a man who was despised and rejected of men. They are promised no salary, holidays or early retirement. They must totally commit their all into their new master's hand. Successful applicants will be expected to devote their gifts, personalities and savings to their new employer. In return they will be given more than they could ever imagine or dream.

Wanted. Real Christians.

For all people

Living God,
We pray for all people:
For those women shut off from a full life
    by tradition and practice.
For those people who are oppressed and exploited.
For those denied their freedom and dignity
    by systems and authorities.
For those forced to leave their homelands
    because of their ideologies.
For those seeking answers and meaning to their lives
    within their own cultures and religions.
For those who labour too long and too hard
    only to barely feed and clothe themselves
    and their families.
For those forced to sell their bodies to survive.
For those women and men who live lives
    of quiet desperation at the hands of the powerful
    and prestigious.
For those and all who suffer
We pray,
Asking that the Church may once again

Give joyful expression to your creative love
Which breaks down barriers
    and unites person to person, woman to man,
    and community to community.
Which gives meaning and hope to empty lives
And makes us reach out to each other
    in generous self-giving.
Which makes us more complete ourselves.
So God,
Fulfil your promise in us
For the sake of all human beings
    through Jesus Christ.

The struggle to put us right

Lord God:
 Take fire and burn our guilt and hypocrisies.
 Take water and wash away the blood which we have
caused to be shed.
 Take hot sunlight and dry the tears of those we have
hurt, and heal their wounded souls, minds and bodies.
 Take love, and root it in our hearts, so that love may
grow, transforming the dry desert of our prejudices and
hatreds.
 Take our imperfect prayers and purify them, so that we
mean what we pray and are prepared to give ourselves to
you along with our words through Jesus Christ our Lord.

Learning to live

No man has learned to live
until he can rise above the narrow confines
of his individualistic concerns
to the broader concerns of all humanity.
Length without breadth
is like a self-contained tributary
having no outward flow to the ocean.
Stagnant, still, and stale,
it lacks both life and freshness.
In order to live creatively
and meaningfully,
our self-concern must be wedded to other concern.

Martin Luther King

We suggest you add the word 'woman' where appropriate.

Bless the 'real' people

O bless this people, Lord, who seek their own face
under the mask and can hardly recognize it . . .
O bless this people that breaks its bond . . .
And with them, all the peoples of North and South,
of East and West,
who sweat blood and sufferings,
and see, in the midst of these millions of waves
the sea swell of the heads of my people
and grant to them warm hands that they may clasp
the earth in a girdle of brotherly hands
beneath the rainbow of thy peace.

Glorify us

The Lord God created us; female and male were we created to live side by side in the image of God.

Parent God, glorify us—each made in your image.

Laws talk of equality of the sexes in terms of pay and opportunity; but give us a vision of equality which transcends that of the human lawmakers.

Parent God, glorify us—each made in your image.

Free us from prejudice about the roles of the sexes, so that every individual may develop his or her full potential. Inspire us to complement each other, but where feminine and masculine together offer the human race fullness and richness.

Parent God, glorify us—each of us made in your image.

Make us aware of what we have done when we deny another's potential by categorising that person in terms of sex.

Parent God, glorify us—each made in your image.

Enable us to seek a greater sensitivity towards one another. Help us to cry when we need to cry, laugh when we need to laugh, and to be angry when we have just cause. Help us not to deny our feelings and emotions; yet to be sensitive to the way our feelings and emotions affect others.

Parent God, glorify us—each of us made in your image.

For the gifts of sex, of manhood and womanhood, we thank you. Parent of the race, lead us constantly to appreciate one another so that female and male, side by side, we may more greatly reflect that glory which is yours.

Parent God, glorify us—each made in your image.

His dying and rising—for us!

Christ our hope:
We give you glory
For the great grace
By which upon the Cross
You stretched out your hands in love
To us all.
By that same grace
Come, risen Saviour,
Into every gesture of unity and fellowship
We make toward one another.
May the peace we share
Be your peace. Amen.

Jamie Wallace

A prayer reflecting the theme of the International Week of Prayer for Christian Unity.

My people, I am your security

In the summer of 1978, David H. Janzen, a member of the New Creation Fellowship in Newton, Kansas, fasted and prayed about a Christian witness against the arms race. He was given what he felt to be a prophecy from the Lord, and shared it with his fellowship, who confirmed it. It was then shared with a group meeting at the Mennonite World Conference held in Wichita, Kansas, in July of that year; that group felt led to share it with the whole general assembly. Following is the prophecy.

My people, proclaim to your governments and your
neighbours that you do not need armaments for your
security.

I am your security. I will give the peacemakers glory as I
defended and glorified my own defenceless son, Jesus.
My kingdom is international.
  I am pleased that my children gather all round the
  globe to give allegiance to one kingdom. My kingdom
  is coming in power.
  No powers, not even the powers of nuclear warfare can
  destroy my kingdom.
My kingdom is from beyond this earth.
  The world thought it had killed Jesus, Jesus through
  whom I have overcome the world. Therefore, be not
  afraid.
You are a gathering of my kingdom;
  My kingdom will last forever.
  Taste the first fruits now;
  Embrace the international fellowship in Christ and
  praise me together.
Do not fear the nuclear holocaust.
  Do not panic or take unloving short cuts to fight the
  armaments monster.
I go before you to do battle.
This is a spiritual battle, the battle to destroy war.
  Do not attempt to fight this battle on your own.
  Fear, guilt and anger will make you spiritual prisoners
  of the enemy if you fight on your own authority.
  Learn to hear my voice. Learn to be at unity with
  those who love me.
  I will lead and protect my army.
  I will coordinate the battle in many nations.
I want to show you where the idols of this age are hidden.
  Learn where are the missile silos, the bomb factories,
  the centres of military command, the prisons for
  dissenters. Understand that those who bow down to
  fear trust in these idols for salvation.
  Stand beside their idols and proclaim my liberating
  kingdom. Invite them to share your life in me.
  Perfect love must be your weapon, for perfect love
  casts out fear.

If you obey my call, you will be persecuted, misunderstood,
powerless.
You will share in my suffering for the world, but I will
never abandon you. You belong to my international,
eternal kingdom.
Do not say time is running out. Do not threaten or despair.
I am the Lord of time. There is not time to seek the
world's approval, but there is time to do what I will lay
before you.
By my mercy I have extended time.
I extended time for a perverse human race when I
called Noah.
I lengthened the time of repentance by sending my
prophets.
I have averted nuclear disaster many times for you.
Jesus offers you all time, time to repent and come to
me. Obey my call and there will be time to do what I
am laying before you.
Now is the time.
I want you to learn who around the world has refused to
bow down to the god of fear or worship weapons of
terror. Hold hands around the world with my soldiers,
my prisoners.
Pray for each other and share my strength with them.
I love those who put their trust in me and I will put
joy in their hearts.
There is time to build my kingdom.
There is time to protest armaments and to build a
spiritual community for those who turn from the idols
of fear.
Call them to join you in the security that flows from
Father, Son, and Spirit, my community, given for you.
My seed is planted in every one of my children;
It is waiting to break the husks of fear that it may grow
toward my son's light.
I did not plant my spirit in Russians or Americans, Arabs
or Israelis, capitalists or communists that they might
destroy each other, but that they might recognize my

40

image in each other and come together in praise of
their creator's name.
My beloved children,
Share the burden of my heart, know my love so that
you may learn to die for one another.
There is time to do this.
Trust me and I will sustain you within my kingdom
forever.

Truth

*At the WCC Assembly in Toronto, Alan Boesak spoke these
powerful words.*

The truth that the Messiah reveals is contrary to the
lies, the propaganda, the idolatrous, the untrustworthy
in the world. His truth is the truth that holds the
freedom and this we are called to proclaim:
It is not true that this world and its people are
doomed to die and be lost . . .
This is true: For God so loved the world that he gave
his only begotten Son, that whosoever believes in him,
shall not perish, but have everlasting life . . .
It is not true that we must accept inhumanity and
discrimination, hunger and poverty, death and
destruction . . .
This is true: I have come that they may have life, and
that abundantly . . .
It is not true that violence and hatred should have the
last word, and that war and destruction have come to
stay forever . . .
This is true: For unto us a child is born, and unto us
a Son is given, and the government shall be upon his

41

shoulder, and his name shall be called wonderful
counsellor, mighty God, the Everlasting Father, the
Prince of peace . . .

It is not true that we are simply victims of the powers
of evil who seek to rule the world . . .

This is true: To me is given all authority in heaven
and on earth, and lo I am with you, even unto the end
of the world . . .

It is not true that we have to wait for those who are
specially gifted, who are the prophets of the Church,
before we can do anything . . .

This is true: I will pour out my Spirit on all flesh,
and your sons and your daughters shall prophesy, your
young men shall see visions, and your old men shall
have dreams . . .

It is not true that our dreams for liberation of
humankind, of justice, of human dignity, of peace are
not meant for this earth and for this history . . .

This is true: The hour comes, and it is now, that the
true worshippers shall worship the Father in spirit and
in truth . . .

Jesus Christ is the life of the world.

Alan Boesak

Lord, guide me

If you try me,
send me out
into the foggy night,
so that I cannot see
my way.

Even if I stumble,
this I beg, that I
may look and smile
serenely,

42

bearing witness
that you are with me
and I walk in peace.

If you try me,
send me out
into an atmosphere
too thin for me to breathe
and I cannot feel the earth
beneath my feet,
let my behaviour
show men that they cannot
part forcibly
from you in whom we
breathe and move
and are.

If you let hate
hamper and trap me,
twist my heart,
disfigure me,
then give my eyes
his love and peace,
my face the expression
of your Son.

Dom Helder Camara

The other Britain

In the 12th Dimbleby Lecture, Bishop David Sheppard
presented with force, clarity, charm and deep feeling, a
disconcerting message from the 'Other Britain' to
'Comfortable Britain', born out of 30 years involvement in
the inner city, which challenged both Government's
assumption that 'there is no other way' and the Church's
complicity in the 'poverty which imprisons the Spirit'.

It was recorded before an invited audience at the Royal Society of Arts, two hundred yards away from Charing Cross Bridge, under whose arches the most destitute of London's 'Other Britons' curl up on the pavement each night in their makeshift cardboard beds. Later, BBC 2's *Newsnight* taped a discussion with some of the audience. Both were transmitted the evening when the Libyan Embassy siege pushed everything else off the air and the main pages of next day's national press. This effectively muted public discussion of the radical challenge of *Good News for the Poor* which David Sheppard powerfully expounded. Two days later the *Daily Telegraph* accused the Bishop of dividing Christians in launching 'a fierce attack on the economic policies of the Government'.

He dealt first with relative poverty, its causes and effects, illustrated with stories of real people in real situations, not statistics from a Government press release. There are 25 year olds, even 35 year olds 'who never had a job'. He spoke of unemployment, bad housing, inadequate education, poor health care, transport, leisure provisions, 'and even policing' as the locked doors of poverty's prison. The 'get on your bike' attitude encouraged the mobility of the self-confident and created 'whole communities of the left-behind'.

Whilst acknowledging his debt to Comfortable Britain, David Sheppard had no option but to criticize that which he loves. 'I am angry when I see the sick human relationships which poverty spawns—depression, deference, fear, cynicism, jealousy and self-righteous blaming.' His challenge to Comfortable Britain was to stand in the shoes of the Other Britain.

David Sheppard next urged that 'poverty is a priority area for us all, especially for Christians'. The concern he was voicing was 'not an expression of off-beat radical theology. It springs out of mainstream Christianity.' He quoted Luke 4, 'The Spirit of the Lord is upon me . . .' and gave as his experience that engagement with poor and needy people threw Christians back on their spiritual resources, for solutions

44

were beyond human endeavour. The Easter faith was about forgiveness through the Cross and hope in a risen, loving Lord. God crucified faces risk, conflict, failure.

Intervention in social and political affairs has a long history in the churches. Not to do so supported an unjust status quo. The anti-slavery campaign, the strictures against usury and the protestant work ethic were illustrations of intervention. The Bishop took issue with Sir Fred Catherwood's exposition of the work ethic and argued that unbridled individualism was not God's way. Our attitude to work should be marked by the transcendent, fraternity and justice. He strongly challenged the free market philosophy and monetarist ideology of the present Government. These policies were producing a 'deep alienation, a dangerous gap between the governors and the governed', resulting in 'a kind of frozen violence' as destructive as the threat of violence on the streets. He challenged the hard faced indifference which ignored the cry of pain 'from the body of our nation'.

In his final section David Sheppard set out four keys to unlock the doors of poverty's prison.

First, 'There is an alternative, several in fact', including a social wage, education and training for all 16–19 years not in jobs, work sharing, a programme of public works. This would involve higher taxation but politicians should 'renounce exploiting the grudging unwillingness of the better off to pay more taxes'.

Second, affirmative action which gives most to those in most need. The rate support grant is one way in which the better off areas of the country help the worse off. Liverpool's £30m cuts should be restored. Pension funds, the grant charitable trusts, business, Government funded research should be encouraged towards areas in decline. To combat racial disadvantage. 'Keep accurate statistics' and 'Accept the principle of positive action'.

Third, support self help, with funds without strings to encourage. 'Centres of resistance to despair' was also the Bishop's vision for inner city churches.

Fourth, work on a basis of partnership and continuity. Policies of confrontation, 'putting the boot in', to the unions when they are weak, provokes long-standing bitterness. We should support the hands of the moderate people who work their hearts out delivering care and concern where it counts.

We are a deeply divided nation. David Sheppard challenged the 'hard heartedness of the educated' in their own interest to combat 'the poverty which imprisons the spirit'. In the ensuing *Newsnight* discussion, the audience was clearly behind the Bishop as he dealt with critics who simply did not understand the history of our cities and whose uncomprehending complacency earned rebuke.

Unless there is a change of heart nationally with practical policies designed to restore dignity to those barely surviving in the Other Britain, then the alternative of 'bloody riots on streets' would have to be faced.

Michael Eastman

Prisoners of conscience

May be read by two, three or more voices

Today, as you walked through the doors of this church to join in the worship, somewhere in the world, the doors closed behind a man or woman in a very different situation. You entered this place to join in the spirit of worship. That unknown person has entered another building to begin a long period of confinement, even terror. He is no thief, no murderer—he may be a doctor, lawyer, teacher, priest, trade unionist, factory worker. Yet he dares to speak his mind, to follow his conscience, and non-violently express his views, his politics, his religion.

All around the world many of these can be treated with great severity. Some are confined to prison, serving long sentences, far in excess of those handed out to criminals. Many are subjected to cruel torture. But we could perhaps find ourselves in the same situation, given different circumstances. Perhaps this very act of worship might, in another country, bring us to prison. We might stay there for years.

How many times have we criticised the Government or dared suggest improvements to their methods? And yet, throughout the world, there are people suffering for their loyalty and for their opinions.

These are the crimes of the 'Prisoners of Conscience'. Today their numbers run into hundreds of thousands. Most of them remain in prison, but it is the privilege and responsibility of Amnesty International to seek out these men and women, making their suffering known to the world and actively to campaign for their release.

Incredible as it is, 2,380 years after Socrates drank hemlock, 1,950 years after the crucifixion of Christ, 445 years after Thomas More was beheaded and 380 years after Giordano Bruno was burnt at the stake, hundreds, thousands of men and women waste away their days in prison for their opinions. But opinions should be free. Let the violent man be guarded, but the man who utters what he thinks must be free, and if he is behind bars it is not he but those who keep him there who are dishonoured.

We who belong to this religious fellowship are seeking ways of supporting the work of Amnesty International. We do this because we believe that as Christians we have to show a practical concern for those who are locked away because of their beliefs. Even if we do not agree wtih their beliefs. For the Christian, there can be no escape from the suffering of man. It is the duty, not the choice, of Christians to fight against injustice. We must enter into the suffering of Jesus as we find it in our brothers.

47

In our comfortable life we can too easily insulate ourselves from the sufferings of the world. It is too easy to gloss: 'If they're in prison, I suppose they've deserved it.' It is too easy to stand by while fellow Christians languish in labour camps for their witness to the Faith. It is too easy to shrink from our Christian responsibility. Christ opted into the Cross.

We build our own walls, prisons of insensitivity condemning ourselves decently to a life apart. Don't condemn yourself to solitary confinement. Break out, release yourself. Pray and work for those Prisoners of Conscience who need our help.

Amnesty International (By kind permission)

His way in confrontation and disputes

The breakdown of the talks in the miners' dispute focused on one word. But let the Church be cautious about ridiculing such a situation. Early Christian councils had great confrontations and conflicts over just one letter! No, there are issues at stake in the words. What is frustrating to most people is the feeling that the two men involved at the heart of these peripatetic and expensive discussions have more than views and opinions to offer.

The Christian Church, as such, cannot break this deadlock. It cannot even do much or so it seems, to influence those involved. Perhaps its best contribution lies in doing all it can to create a climate of opinion in which the nation will not stand for such costly and, at times, comical caperings from London to Edinburgh and back and places in between. So let the Church proclaim more and more the unifying elements in life. They do not seem to appeal to the politicians who wallow in party confrontation, but deep in

48

the heart of 'the common people' everywhere there *is* the longing for harmony.

And all the wickedness of the world, expressed in violence, hijacks, terrorist activities, murders and rapes, do not deny those deep-seated desires. The reality is that we have a global village, that national barriers, in the jet-age, become much more of an irrelevance, that people from all walks of society meet and mingle, do the same things, enjoy the same leisure activities.

The Church must help the nations to move from the theme of confrontation to the theme of harmony, the harmony of humanity with its home (the ecological movement is one of the expressions of this theme; and concern over nuclear arms another), the harmony of humanity itself (ecumenism, racial integration, family), harmony with time (retreat and the escape from stress), inner harmony (integration, wholeness).

And the Church has the way to harmony to proclaim. It is the way of the Lord.

Editorial in The Church of England Newspaper/British Weekly

Greater love hath no man than this

We suggest a number of readers are used. Here is a story of suffering and grief. And yet, hope is still found. Saturday, December 19, 1981, the Penlee lifeboat from Mousehole, Cornwall was launched to aid a stricken Irish coaster, the Union Star. *A raging south-west storm hampered the rescue effort. Disaster struck and eight lifeboat men, led by their coxswain Trevelyan Richards, lost their lives, as did five men, a woman and two teenage girls on the* Union Star.

The grief of Christmas Eve poured out to overflowing at the funeral service that morning of Coxwain Trevelyan

Richards. Many of the mourners who had packed the Paul*
Parish Church long before the funeral was due to begin,
broke down and wept openly as the cortege came in.

In a church whose flame of faith has survived burning by
the Spaniards and bombing by the Germans, this must rank
among the most emotional moments in its long history.
Grief was perhaps most poignant among those who may
never be granted the mercy of seeing their menfolk laid to
rest.

The people of Mousehole were there, feeling personally
the pain of mourning.

With arms linked, and heads bowed, eight men of Penlee,
the replacement crew of the lifeboat, wearing their RNLI
jerseys with pride, carried the coffin of their skipper. Two
others walked in front, and another behind, while the coffin
iteself was covered by the RNLI flag. On top was a huge
cross of red flowers and a coxwain's peaked cap. Before the
bearers came the Vicar, the Rev High Cadman, Rural Dean
and Chaplain of Penlee branch, together with the Assistant
Bishop, Brother Michael, the Suffragan Bishop of St
Germans.

'I am the Resurrection and the Life . . .' said Rev
Cadman and the huge congregation rose. The funeral
procession had to weave its way through the church for
hundreds stood inside when every seat had been taken . . .

Brother Michael quoted from Charles Causley's 'Sailor's
Carol' and commented: 'We shall always remember that
this season of goodwill and peace on earth, was also a season
of pain and sorrow.'

He said the spirit of service was one of the noblest
elements in man. 'We honour and recognise it as something
that can never be lost.' Like eternal truths of love,
compassion and care, it was a gift of God and beyond
words.

They gave thanks to God, and prayed for the men,

---

* Mousehole is in the Parish of Paul. In the village there is no
Anglican Church. Paul is half a mile from Mousehole harbour.

recognising those two moments in life of which they could all be certain, of birth and death.

Brother Michael added that there were no adequate words with which to express their desire to share in their grief and in their glory . . .

The Rev Cadman, who had been so deeply involved in the heartbreak of the village since Saturday's tragedy, and helping through the long night of Saturday and the heartbreak of Sunday, to bring strength to the bereaved, said that Mr Richards had been coxswain of the Penlee boat for 11 years and in the lifeboat service for 30 years . . .

'Like the rest of the lifeboat crews he pressed on regardless. He was quite prepared to face the fierce seas, the vicious seas, particularly in order to save lives.

'He and his crew, seven other seamen, fine men all, lost their lives, they gave their lives in order to save their fellows, even when they were strangers,' Mr Cadman declared.

He added that they also remembered those who lost their lives on the coaster, *Union Star*, that night. 'Greater love has no man than this, that a man lay down his life for his friends.'

The call of the sea, the call to venture, and venturing, the call to the need of one's fellows, were all compelling motives. The call sign SOS—a call to Save Our Souls, which was more than our bodies. The immediate reaction was the the RNLI men would answer the call to the death. They learned to take the rough waves with the smooth.

Their death, for the sake of others, was electric in its effect on other people as they heard the news. It seemed to act as a catalyst and people had responded around the world. 'We thank God for the courage and kingliness which cause men to risk all for love's sake,' he said. This was what it really meant to love one's fellow man.

In a world which had become very selfish, and very fond of money, there had been an enormous response as they heard of this tragedy.

Mr Cadman spoke of a letter from Cambridge, which had

51

been received locally, and on the envelope of which had been written: 'our prayers and sympathy go out to the village of Mousehole from the sorting office at Cambridge . . .'

'So we offer the Gospel of hope in this old church, of Jesus Christ on the Cross, God in it all, also with us, in His strength of faith and love which cannot and will not let us go.'

They mourned the passing of brave men. Mr Richards and his comrades, and they sought Christ's love and solace. To the Christian there was always the certainty of the morning. Living on in faith they would find Christ would lead them out of the valley of deep darkness to the sunny uplands of God's love and promise of fulfilment. 'This is what we are thinking about today, until the day breaks and the shadows flee away. We have the faith and assurance, and on this we stand, come wind and come weather.'

Following the hymn of the seamen 'Eternal Father, Strong To Save', prayers by Mr Cadman, and the Blessing by Brother Michael, the cortege left the church to the hymn 'The Old Rugged Cross'.

But that night, around the harbour front of Mousehole, the Christmas lights shone out. They were switched on again, after being in darkness since the tragedy, at the request of the bereaved wives so that the children might see them. The lifeboat men themselves had worked hard to make them such a success and one of their number, Mr Charles Greenhaugh, had switched them on the night before the disaster.

On Christmas Eve there was a new centrepiece. On the hillside above the village shone over Mount's Bay the Cross, with an angel on each side, a message of goodwill to the people of West Cornwall whose thoughts and prayers were with them at this time.

R. Douglas Williams

The fisherman's psalm

The Lord is my Pilot: I shall not drift,
He lighteth me across the dark waters:
He steereth me in deep channels.
He keepeth my log:
He guideth me by the star of holiness
For His Name's sake.
Yea, though I sail mid the thunders and tempests,
I will dread no danger: for Thou art near me;
Thy love and Thy care they shelter me.
Thou preparest a harbour before me in the homeland
    of eternity:
Thou anointest the waves with oil: my ship rideth
    calmly.
Surely sunlight and starlight shall favour me on the
    voyage I take:
And I will rest in the port of my God for ever.

The arms race

*This is a mimed skit performed by two clowns (or possibly by
two teams of clowns, working in relay fashion). The skit is
improved by suitable taped background music (which helps
draw a crowd when working on the street, and also to focus
their attention) and music-hall type signs, held up between
sections.*

*Props: taped music and portable tape player, three lettered
signs: THE BIG RACE, ARMS BUILD-UP, STAR
WARS; a large pile of arms—shaped out of polystyrene,
cardboard, etc (a supply of arms from store window dummies is*

really *effective and funny); in a large box—blindfolds, short sticks with 'eyes' on top, two telephone receivers connected with red string.*

First sign THE BIG RACE is displayed.
At the start of the skit two clowns execute a series of drill steps to the martial music, gradually becoming more and more independent and out of step. The race 'starts' as one and then the other takes the arms out of the box and carries them to a pile in their own corner. When the music stops (after not a little cheating and pushing around) each clown or team counts up on their fingers the number of their arms.
Second sign ARMS BUILD-UP is displayed.
The second piece of music begins with an 'On your mark, Get set, Go!!'
The clowns line up and set off with a racing start to take arms from their individual piles and stack them one on top of another in a great mound in the middle (under which have been preplaced the red cord and, nearby, the television receivers). The build-up continues until a proper wall is formed between the two sides. When the music stops, through mime, the clowns indicate the impossibility of seeing or contacting the other side.
Third sign STAR WARS is displayed.
At the appropriate theme music, the blindfolds go on and the two sides mime scooping up, hurling, batting back and forth across the 'wall' and finally deflecting out into the audience 'space' objects, until one is missed and not deflected. This coincides pretty well with the build-up of the music and provides a good background for the clown who 'missed' to pull off his blindfolds, wave frantically over the wall, and attempt to reach the other side on the red 'phone'. The attempt is too late however, and at the climax of the music the clowns pull over the wall with the connecting string of the telephone causing an explosion which topples the wall and causes the clowns to fall down 'dead'.

A last sign THE END may be displayed.

Note: We offer this as an idea which may be implemented whole or improved upon to suit individual situations. We've caused laughs and provoked discussion with our arms race . . . an improvisational game based upon use of our own arms— arms tied behind our backs, arm-mies, long arm of the law, out of arm's reach, etc.—can loosen up a group to try this skit.

Sandra Pollerman
'Nibbles and Clown and Flym' from **The Holy Fools**

A little advice

Seeing the state of the nations, he went up on the mountain and when he sat down the world leaders came to him. And he opened his mouth and taught them through the mass media, saying: 'You have heard that it was said, "An eye for an eye and a tooth for a tooth." But I say to you, Why stop there? Resist one who is evil. If anyone strikes you on the right cheek, have you not cause enough to smash his face in? If anyone would sue you and take your coat, get your lawyers on to it immediately and take him to court, for generosity is a sign of weakness. You have heard that it used to be said, "You shall love your neighbour and hate your enemy." But I say to you, Hate your neighbours also and be suspicious of their intentions; what good is trust in this day and age? For if you love those who love you, you have only yourself to blame when things turn nasty. Does not everyone do the same? Therefore, be selfish, that the whole world might be selfish.'

If I speak in the tongues of men and of angels, but have not aggression, I am a namby pamby and a windy wet-legs. And if I have political powers and understand all problems, both social and economic, and if I enter all disputes, but have not aggression, I am nothing. If I cling onto all my possessions and protect myself at all costs, without aggression, I am done for. Aggression is fruitless and harsh; aggression is not humble or caring, but arrogant and rude. Aggression always insists on its own way, avoiding discussion or compromise. It is proud and strong; it lashes out at once when its interests are threatened and rejoices at another's defeat. Aggression hurts all things, tramples all things, breaks all things, destroys all things. Aggression always ends in tears. So hate, greed, and aggression abide, these three; but the greatest of these is aggression.

Paul Burbridge

Sunday morning

A man at the store
Just told me that
This was the end of the world.

I suppose he was
Referring to the state
Of our morals
And the lack of
Attention to
Old Testament prophecies.

I suppose he was
Versed in
Revelation
Even more than
Arabian oil.

I suppose
It had been
Revealed
To him and

Several others
Who are always
Nameless.

A man at the store
Just told me that
This was the end of the world.

No, Sir.
This is Durham.
And it's almost
Spring.

Conrad Weiser

Easy come—easy go

They make it all too easy,
    some of these preacher guys,
They seem in competition,
    I appear to be the prize.
They plead for my reaction,
    tell me I must raise a hand.
In order that I might attain
    their Ever-Happy-Land!
They say it's straightforward,
    it's as plain as ABC,
There's nothing really to it,
    it is pure simplicity.
If I want to be blissful
    and be free from all my woe,

I just 'Turn on to Jesus'
    and I watch my worries go.
I walk out at a meeting,
    or I throw aside restraint,
Or I smile because God loves me,
    and, Bingo I'm a saint!
But what would happen really,
    if I follow what they say?
I doubt that very little
    would occur their 'easy' way.
Well, a walk would exercise my legs,
    a smile might give me charm,
A raise hand slow my pulse-rate
    as the blood drains from my arm.
My name has been recorded
    by a dozen preacher men,
But all that's worked in practice
    is my plastic ballpoint men.
These preachers seem nomadic,
    and their visits hit-and-miss,
I took a look at Jesus
    and He didn't work like this.
He laid down preconditions
    and He wasn't on the make,
The terms of His discipleship
    are very tough to take.
He spoke of self-denial,
    which makes Him the only Boss;
He promised persecution,
    spoke of taking up a cross.
He told the folk who'd listen
    that they had a price to pay!
Why do some preachers
    water down what Jesus had to say?

Gordon Bailey

Seeing is believing?

Characters: a woman (W); her friend, male or female (F); an intruder, a male or female (I).

W: I'm a very modern person
F: in a scientific age
W: and I only believe what I can see
F: or touch
W: see or touch
F: or handle.
W: That's the same as touch.
F: O.K.
W: I only believe what I can see or touch.
I: Like electricity, for example.
W: Don't interrupt . . .
I: But you can't see electricity . . .
W: That's not the point.
I: It's very much the point.
W: Will you please mind your own business?
I: Sorry, but I thought . . .
W: As I was saying, being a very modern person
F: in a scientific age . . .
I: If you really are being scientific you will have to admit that either you don't believe in electricity, or that there are some things you can't see but which you do believe in.
W: I don't know who you are, but will you please go away. Now, as I was saying, I only believe what I can see
F: or touch
W: or touch. Therefore, when someone comes along with a story of a man who died . . .
F: in front of everyone
W: and was duly certified dead by the authorities
F: and buried
W: Dead and buried, and a massive stone rolled over the mouth of the tomb

F: Massive!

W: and sealed

F: and watched

W: and a surveillance kept by properly authorised military personnel

F: and guarded by soldiers.

W: That's what I said.

F: Sorry.

W: Now when someone tells me that this man is alive again, I say I will not believe them unless I see him

F: and touch him

W: and touch him

I: Excuse me.

W: You again!

I: Me again. Do you believe in Australia?

W: Of course I do.

F: Of course she does.

I: Have you ever seen it?

W: No.

F: Or touched it?

W: Be quiet!

F: Sorry.

I: Then why do you believe in it?

W: Because I have been told it is there.

I: I have been told that Jesus is alive

W: Told by someone reliable?

F: Yes, someone reliable.

I: Someone reliable.

W: Like who?

I: My friend Terry.

W: Terry Smith!

F: Smithy!

I: Yes.

W: I don't believe a word he says.

F: Nor me.

I: Nor me—once. He's changed.

F: Changed?

W: You'll be telling me next he's become a Christian.

60

I: He has.

W: Terry!?

F: Smithy!?

I: Sure.

W: Convince me.

I: Go and see for yourself. He's changed all right. Go and see.

F: See or touch

W: Be quiet. But I can't stay here arguing with you. I must get my children's supper.

F: Yes, she must.

I: Why?

W: Because they're hungry.

I: Let them starve!

W: What a horrible suggestion

F: Disgraceful.

I: Why bother with them? What do they mean to you?

W: I love them.

F: Yes, she does

I: Love! But you don't believe in love.

W: Of course I believe in love.

F: Of course she does.

I: Have you ever *seen* love?

W: What a stupid question!

I: Or touched it?

W: Don't be ridiculous. I must go. Goodnight.

F: Cheers!

I: God bless you.

John Horner

Enjoying a lifestyle

Giving is important. Even more important is *living justly*.
Some people have found that considering world needs in
the light of the Word of God has affected their whole way of
life. Life had become more purposeful and satisfying,
simpler, healthier, and more just, by taking action in these
and other ways:

- working for world justice, peace and disarmament
- seeking justice for various people with grievances in
  our own society
- talking of One World and opposing racism in conversation
- improving the environment, socially and physically
- preserving wild life and natural beauty
- conserving fuel and other limited resources
- saving grain and reducing health risks by cutting out
  excessive meat-eating
- keeping luxuries in check

What makes a home?

What makes a perfect home?
Look at the adverts; pick up a magazine,
They will tell you.
For a perfect home you need:
a washing machine, a dish washing machine, electric tin-
opener, food mixer, refrigerator, deep freeze, Venetian
blinds, velvet curtains, fitted carpets, vacuum cleaner,
carpet cleaner, carpet sweeper, colour television,
transistor radio, central heating, telephone, cocktail
cabinet, guest room, sheepskin rug, fitted wardrobes,
electric blankets, place mats, stainless steel cutlery, and of
course . . . Daz, Persil, Omo, Lux, Ariel, Fairy Snow. A

mum who uses Fairy Liquid, and a Bank Manager in the
wardrobe.

It's all bigger than our small world

Our pilgrimage to a larger Christ, demands, above all, that
we listen to the hitherto stifled voices of our brothers and
sisters in Africa, Asia and Latin America. Whether it be in
the witness of Liberation Theology, in the struggle for
justice, in the search for peace, in the experience of women,
the Gospel calls us to choose life and to work for the
realization of the Kingdom of God in our world
community.

We may wish to contest what we hear, and what we hear
may initially induce conflict in us, or even be at odds with
what we believe about Christ. We must be prepared to be
told that our listening is too late, too slow or too passive:
that the situation is desperate and we are denying Christ,
even seeking to thwart Him, by what we do to one another.

*Words used as part of an invitation to students to attend a
conference In Search Of A Larger Christ that was held in
Edinburgh in 1985.*

Prayer for forgiveness

Where we've gone haywire
The hatred which divides nation from nation,
    race from race, class from class,
Father, forgive.

The covetous desire of men and nations
    to possess what is not their own,
Father, forgive.

The greed which exploits the labours of men,
    and lays waste the earth,
Father, forgive.

Our envy of the welfare and happiness of others,
Father, forgive.

Our indifference to the plight of the homeless
    and the refugee,
Father, forgive.

The lust which uses for ignoble ends the bodies
    of men and women,
Father, forgive.

The pride which leads us to trust in ourselves
    and not in God,
Father, forgive.

Coventry Cathedral Prayer, 1964.

PART THREE

Words of Hope and Vision

Notes on Part Three extracts

The dream. Rely on the spirit and tone of the passage and do not try to pretend you are addressing a large rally: The Luther King event has happened and cannot be repeated realistically outside of competent theatrical backcloths. So, whether one or several readers are employed, take things naturally allowing the rhythm and mood to slowly build the pace throughout. Perhaps preface it by singing a familiar spiritual—Nobody Knows the Trouble I've Seen—or a song from the Civil Rights Movement.

Don't dance on the wire. This can be taken on different levels, either as a poem about two people's relationship or as about the Christian life, lived in the spirit of Jesus and encountering the unusual and unexpected. Can be read by one voice throughout or several voices can be added for the chorus/refrain.

A world without tears. The reader can stop at the end of some lines while the leader briefly enlarges on the point being made from the relevant scripture passage.

The dream

Dr Martin Luther King, Jr put his life at risk in saying this dream can come true.

'I say to you today even though we face the difficulties of today and tomorrow, I still have a dream. It is a dream that is deeply rooted in the American dream. I have a dream that one day this nation will rise up, live out the true meaning of its creed. We hold these truths to be self-evident, that all men are created equal.

'I have a dream that one day on the red hills of Georgia the sons of former slaves and the sons of former slaveowners will be able to sit down together at the table of brotherhood. I have a dream that one day even the state of Mississippi, a state sweltering with the heat of oppression, will be transformed into an oasis of freedom and justice.

'I have a dream that my four little children one day will live in a nation where they will not be judged by the colour of their skin, but by the content of their character.

'I have a dream that one day every valley shall be exalted, every hill and mountain shall be made low. The rough places will be made plain and the crooked places will be made straight. This is the faith that I go back to the South with. With this faith we will be able to hew out of the mountains of despair the stone of hope. With this faith we will be able to work together, to pray together, to struggle together, to go to jail together, to stand up for freedom together, knowing we will be free one day.

'This will be the day when all of God's children will be able to sing with new meaning "Let freedom ring". So let freedom ring from the prodigious hilltops of New Hampshire; let freedom ring from the mighty mountains of New York. But not only that. Let freedom ring from Stone Mountain of Georgia. Let freedom ring from every hill and molehill of Mississippi, from every mountain-side.

'When we allow freedom to ring from every town and hamlet, from every state and every city, we will be able to speed up that day when all of God's children, black men and white men, Jews and Gentiles, Protestants and Catholics, will be able to join hands and sing in the words of an old Negro spiritual, "Free at last! Free at last! Great God A'mighty, we are free at last!"'

Martin Luther King, Jr

Don't dance on the wire

Can you take what I give you
Will you pay what I'm worth
Will you gamble your diamonds
For a handful of earth
When you're used, bruised and bewildered
Will you say you didn't really mind
Can you love someone who's likely
To seem capricious and unkind?

   chorus
    Don't dance on the wire if you can't hear the beat
    Don't stand near the fire if you don't want the hot-seat
    Don't gamble with real money if you wanna stay real neat
    And if you don't like flying, don't get swept off your feet.

Would you risk your reputation
For a few hours next to my heart
Do you feel a sense of elation
When you play the lovers part
Would you risk the swollen river

Will you work until you bleed
Will you give your undivided attention
To the loving that I need?

chorus etc

Don't say I didn't warn you
Don't say you didn't know
Don't say I should have told you
How far you'd need to go
Don't say that now you're sorry
Don't say that now you see
You'll have to share what I've been through
if you want to live your dreams with me. . . .

© *Vince Cross 1983*

New people and new paths

FIRST READING (Jeremiah 7 and Deuteronomy 30)

Reader 1: Bible speech is centred in action and movement.
To walk the way God commanded was to walk the right
way and to move in the right direction. To follow his
leading was to be loyal in moving forward: 'I will be
your God, and you shall be my people; and walk in all
the way that I command you, that it may be well with
you' (Jeremiah 7:23).

Reader 2: Let us speak of the people of the Way and of the
paths they follow:

Reader 3: 'See, I have set before you this day life and good,
death and evil. If you obey the commandments of the
Lord your God which I command you this day, by

loving the Lord your God, by walking in his ways . . . then you shall live . . . and the Lord your God will bless you. . . . I have set before you LIFE and death, blessing and curse; therefore, choose life, that you and your descendents may LIVE' (Deuteronomy 30:15–19, emphasis added).

Reader 1: Therefore choose life—that YOU may live.

Reader 2: Life and good, death and evil. CHOOSE life.

Reader 3: Love God, walk in his ways, choose LIFE.

Reader 1: Therefore

Reader 2: Therefore

Reader 3: Therefore

All: Therefore, choose life, choose to be alive, choose to live in the Way. Choose life that:

Reader 1: you (*echo*) may (*shout*) LIVE!

Reader 2: You

Reader 3: You

SECOND READING (Psalm 8, emphasis added)

Reader 1: 'O Lord, our Lord,
how majestic is thy name in all the earth! . . .
When I look at thy heavens, the work of thy
fingers,
the moon and the stars which thou hast
established;
what is man that thou art mindful of HIM . . . ?'

Reader 2: When I look at the bigness of moon and stars, (*disdainfully*) WHAT IS MAN?

Reader 3 (*questioningly*): What IS man? Why care for him?

Reader 1 (*softly, but with intensity*): Why is man important? What are we to God? WHAT is man? (*echo*)

Reader 2: What IS man?

Reader 3: What is MAN?

Reader 1: And yet, and 'YET thou hast made him little less
than God,
and dost crown him with glory and honour.

71

Thou hast given him dominion over the works of
 thy hands;
 . . . the beasts of the field,
 the birds of the air, and the fish of the sea.'

Reader 2: So there WE are—little less than God—crowned
with glory and honour—in CHARGE of fields, fowl, and
fish.

Reader 3: That's US? That's not exactly a description of
Un-response/ability!

All: What is man? What are WE? (*elongated*) In-n-n Charge!
Co-creator with the Creator. (*forcefully*) Responsible!

Reader 1 (*with anguish, fear*): Oh, Lord!

Reader 2 (*factually*): O Lord—OUR Lord, OUR Lord!

All (*slowly*): O Lord . . .

Reader 1: Our Lord,

Reader 2: My Lord,

Reader 3: Your Lord,

All: 'OUR LORD! How majestic is thy name in ALL the
earth!'

THIRD READING (Isaiah 43:15–19, emphasis added)

Reader 1: 'I am the Lord, your Holy One,
 the Creator of Israel, your King.'
 Thus says the Lord,
 who makes a WAY in the sea,
 a PATH in the mighty waters. . . .
 'Remember not the former things,
 nor consider the things of old.
 BEHOLD, I am doing a new thing;
 now it springs forth, do you not perceive it?
 I will make a way in the wilderness
 and rivers in the desert.'

Reader 2: Here and now new things are being done. They
are springing forth in surprising places.

Reader 3: Can we see them? Can we perceive their
importance?

All: Think of it—WAYS EVEN, even through the wilderness!

Reader 1 (*quietly, but with intensity*): the confusion,

Reader 2: the uncertainty,

Reader 3: the indecision,

Reader 1: the wondering,

Reader 2: the trying,

Reader 3: the apathy,

All: the WIL-DER-NESS. And PATHS, steps to follow, PATHS in the barren

　　Reader 1: barren (*echo*) desert.

　　Reader 2 (*echo*): barren

　　All (*loud, triumphant*): A new THING, let US SEE, ways in the wilds, paths in the wasteland, Aaa-MEN! New ways to walk!

FOURTH READING (*Matthew 5, emphasis added*)

Reader 1: 'You have heard that it was said, "An eye for an eye, and a tooth for a tooth." But now I tell you: do not take revenge on someone who does you wrong. If anyone slaps you on the right cheek, let him slap your left cheek too. And if someone takes you to court to sue you for your shirt, let him have your coat as well. And if any one forces you to go one mile, go with him *two miles*' (Matthew 5:38–40, TEV; 5:41, RSV).

Reader 2: New ways to walk.

Reader 3: Walking the second mile, walking WITH—

All: 'Love your enemies, and pray for those who mistreat you' (Matthew 5:44, TEV).

Reader 1: That's more than what's expected—that's doing the 'special'.

Reader 2: No revenge. Much caring.

All: Loving, walking along the second mile, a new way of walking, new people.

Reader 3: 'When anyone is joined to Christ he is a new being: the old is gone, the new has come.

Reader 1: 'All this is done by God, who through Christ

73

changed us from enemies into his friends, and gave us the task of making others his friends also.

Reader 2: 'Our message is that God was making friends of all men through Christ . . . he has given us the message of how he makes them his friends.

Reader 3: 'Here we are, then, speaking for Christ, as though God himself were appealing to you through us: On Christ's behalf (*slowly*) WE BEG YOU,

All: 'Let God change you from enemies into friends!'

(2 Corinthians 5:17–20, TEV, emphasis added.)

(*Repeat two more times with increasing intensity*)

Reader 1: So the request, the invitation is: Walk in THE WAY.

Reader 2: NEW people need NEW paths.

Reader 3: There are choices—choose life!

Reader 1: Good life.

Reader 2: Warm life.

Reader 3: Loving life.

All: Walking along WITH LIFE.

Reader 1: What is man?

All: What are we?

Reader 2: In charge of the paths of earth, sea, and sky.

All: God's majestic earth!

Reader 1: Doing/Being/Becoming new.

Reader 2: Joined with Christ.

Reader 3: Walk two miles.

Reader 1: Give your coat.

Reader 2: Enemies are friends.

All: Can you see it, can you do it? It's a good new thing: a new path for new ways for all.

Reader 1: New

Reader 2: New

Reader 3: New

All (*intense, quiet*): People, (*shout*) YES!

Richard D. Orr

We live in hope

Reader 1: At Christmas we speak readily of the COMING of the one who brings PEACE and HOPE. Such a season should not be relegated to a few frantic days. It is a fresh festive time. People smile with anticipations they can't keep to themselves. Handmade and home-prepared surprises are shared with great warmth and festivity. Secrets are special. The message: the Christ has come, the kingdom is HERE! Let us spin our hopes about the coming.

Reader 2: I hope he comes with HEALING:
—I need putting back together.
—I need wholeness for my fragments.
—I need energy for my wastedness.
—I need quiet strength for my tired body.

All: COME, O COME.

Reader 2: I hope he comes with DREAMING:
—I like imagination.
—I like dreams to fill me with joy.
—I need a vision to give me hope.
—I want an 'inkling' of hope for those impossible dreams.
—I hope he comes with a soaring, curious, all-things-are-possible imagination, a HURRAH of expectation, THE reason to try and try and try—

All: COME, O COME.

Reader 4: I hope he comes letting us know that PEOPLE are a FULL-TIME JOB!
—I'm tired of tasks.
—I'm tired of grinding up new energies for more doing, doing, doing.
—I'm tired of measuring and naming my days by how many jobs I got done.
—Is that heaven? Finishing all your jobs?
—I'm tired of missing people because I'm paralysed with my list of stuff to do.

All: COME, O COME.

Reader 5: I hope he comes with an end to aloneness.
  —People are afraid of themselves.
  —We're professionals at hiding from one another.
  —WHY IS IT EASIER TO BE HARD THAN TENDER?
  —Why do we think our hurting is weakness?
Reader 1: I hope he comes, freeing us to embrace.
Reader 2: Why is hugging people weird?
Reader 3: I hope he invites us to make an impact—letting us be able to hug.
Reader 4: I hope that crying and laughing and confessing and longing for—can all be a part of the whole and holy human WAY.
Reader 1: I want to be loved.
Reader 2: I want to be appreciated for what I AM.
Reader 3: I want to know the richness people are—without judgments about properness or rightness.
Reader 4: People ARE/and people are lovable!
Reader 5: Wouldn't that be GOOD NEWS!
Reader 1: You're not alone.
Reader 2: Your pieces are going to come together.
Reader 3: Body is OK.
Reader 4: Mind can imagine.
Reader 5: Feelings are acceptable.
All: You are ONE, your spirit can be ALIVE. You BELONG.
  COME, O COME
Reader 1: King of vision,
Reader 2: Lord of aliveness,
Reader 3: Spirit of possibility,
Reader 4: Babe of holding love,
All: COME, come to us.
Reader 5: Light our dark streets.
Reader 1: Love us.
Reader 2: Open us.
All: COME!
All: Amen.

Richard D. Orr

We have a dream

A Litany

Leader: Almighty God, that your church may become a prophetic witness for peace,
People: We have a dream.
Leader: That we no longer neglect the world's poor and needy,
People: We have a dream.
Leader: That we may halt the present moves towards war,
People: We have a dream.
Leader: That we may stop our threats to use nuclear weapons,
People: We have a dream.
Leader: That we may rely only on the armour of truth, faithfulness, love and the word of God,
People: We have a dream.
Leader: That we build a world for love and human family,
People: We have a dream.
Leader: That we may hope in the face of despair and brokenness,
People: We have a dream.
Leader: That we may grow in faith and awareness of the resurrection at work within us,
People: We have a dream.

A song of hope, a song of love

Refrain
Rejoice, my brothers (sisters),
    he's with us still,
Hope now risen is all around us.

A song of hope is all we need,
 A song of love for all to heed.
Refrain

Hope is the cloud on which we stand
Knowing it will pervade the land.

Hope is the message we sing for you
Help us Lord, please make us true.

A song of love isn't hard to find
For a song of love brings hope to mind.

Celebrate hope, receive hope, give hope.
Jesus Christ is here, sing it out.

*Sing to the tune of the spiritual All My Trials, Lord, Soon Be
Over.*

Second coming

It is not for us
to define the day.
But he will come
and men (women) will once again be called
to proclaim the word of God
in such a way
that it will change and renew the world.

Dietrich Bonhoeffer

A world without tears

Just think of a world without tears
Where a man can live for a million years (John 17:3)
With never a grief, an ache or a pain (Isaiah 33:24)
And never a thought of dying again (Revelation 21:34)

Think of a world, when a man plants a vine (Micah 4:4)
He can sit in its shade and say 'This is mine'
He will live in the house his own hand has made,
And naught shall molest, or make him afraid (Isaiah 65:21,22)

Think of a world without bloodshed and strife
Where no man dare take another man's life (Micah 4:3)
Where man unto man will unite in peace (Isaiah 9:7)
And malice and hatred for evermore cease. (Susanna 2:14)

Think of the earth as a global paradise (Isaiah 35:12)
Where mountain and desert will dazzle your eyes.
With beautiful flowers and shrubbery and trees,
With gay butterflies, song birds and bees. (Isaiah 66:1, 60:13)

Think! Just as sure as God's word is the Truth (John 17:17)
A man shall return to the days of his youth (Job 33:25,
    Isaiah 33:24)
His flesh shall become as the flesh of a child (Matthew 5:5)
And the words that he speaks will be cheerful and mild.

Think of a world where a lame man will leap
From crag to crag like a deer or a sheep (Isaiah 35:5,6)
Where none will be deaf, and none will be blind
And the dumb shall speak and speak forth his mind.

Think of a world where each man is his brother (Matthew
    23:8)
Not esteeming himself above that of another (Jeremiah 31:34)
Where man unto man will be friend to friend (John 15:14,15)
In a world without tears, that will never end.

Think of a world where the dead will have risen (John
    5:28,29)
From their silent Tombs that held them in prison.
To for ever live to love and caress (Mark 5:35, 5:38–42)
Their loved ones, and friends in righteousness (Luke 7:11–16)

Now a world without tears is not just a dream.
As many persons might make it seem (Revelation 21:5,6)
For just as sure as the Bible is true (Hebrews 6:18)
A world without tears now lies before you. (Luke 21:28)

And since such a world before you now lies (Luke 31:31)
Wouldn't you like to live in this Paradise? (Isaiah 66:17)
And share all the blessings that God has in store (Psalm
    72:7,8)
For all who will do His will evermore. (Matthew 6:10)

Good news of the Kingdom is still being sung (Matthew
    24:14)
Throughout every nation, Kingdom and tongue.
And all who are thirsting for truth are invited (Luke 12:32)
To join the New Order, and thus be united. (John 10:16)

In praising our God, our saviour and king (Jeremiah 10:10)
We give to Him all we have—everything (Psalm 93:1)
That we might live throughout endless years (2 Peter 3:13)
In a world without sorrow—a world without tears. (Isaiah
    25:8)

PART FOUR

Words for Christmas and Easter

Notes on Part Four extracts

Obviously many times and seasons could have been chosen for this section but Christmas and Easter seem the two times that really unite Christians.

See, hear and know it! Why not put up on the walls cuttings from journals and newspapers, magazines and books that display the sentiments expressed in this proclamation? Then have someone point to each as the gathering recites the appropriate lines.

Messianic blues. This might be part of a general look at how Jesus is seen by different groups of people today. Compare these with the witness of the first Christians.

Easter prayer. This needs different voices as it is rather long to be read by one person. The last lines from 'And so we ask . . .' can be said by all, with plenty of life.

Jesus is alive. This might be prefaced by pointing out that the 'greats' of various times and occasions have often been forgotten or at best, remembered merely as an historical exercise. Jesus is different—He lives today and changes individuals and societies.

One solitary life. This can be written out in the form of a poster on a large visual display sheet and read by the whole gathering. Alternatively, one person can read it and add a personal testimony of how Christ has changed his/her life.

Christmas

Heavenly Father, as we sing our Christmas-time praise our
    own words condemn us.
We are thanking you for sending Jesus to show us how life
    ought to be lived; but we have not often really tried
    to live like Him.
        Forgive us, Father.

See, hear and know it!

There is dignity here
    we will exalt it.
There is courage here
    we will support it.
There is humanity here
    we will enjoy it.
There is a universe in every child
    we will share in it.
There is a voice calling through the
    chaos of our times;
there is a spirit moving across the
    waters of our world;
there is movement,
    a light,
    a promise of hope.
Let them that have eyes to see,
    see
Let them that have ears to hear,
    hear
        But
    look not for Armageddon,
nor listen for a trumpet.

Behold, we bring you good tidings of great joy:
The Incarnation.

Philip Andrews, Australia
Suffering and Hope, Christian Conference of Asia

Christmas—for others

We pray for the old and lonely people this Christmas.

They are those who greet silent streets with fear and
   apprehension.

They are those who will lose their regular daily visitor
   —the postman and the milkman;
those who will lay table for the very first time, just for
   themselves;
those who will read and re-read the precious letter and
   Christmas card . . .

We pray for the old and lonely people this Christmas.

Tony Jasper

Sharon's Christmas prayer

She was five
sure of the facts,
and recited them
with slow solemnity,
convinced every word
was revelation.
She said

they were so poor
they had only peanut butter and jelly sandwiches
to eat
and they went a long way from home
without getting lost. The lady rode
a donkey, the man walked, and the baby
was inside the lady.
They had to stay in a stable
with an ox and an ass (hee-hee)
but the Three Rich Men found them
because a star lighted the roof.
Shepherds came and you could
pet the sheep but not feed them.
Then the baby was borned.
And do you know who he was?
    Her quarter eyes inflated
    to silver dollars.
The baby was God.
    And she jumped in the air,
    whirled round, dived into the sofa,
    and buried her head under the cushion
    which is the only proper response
    to the Good News of the Incarnation.

John Shea

Mary's song

Blue homespun and the bend of my breast
keep warm this small hot naked star
fallen to my arms. (Rest . . .
you who have had so far
to come.) Now nearness satisfies
the body of God sweetly. Quiet he lies
whose vigor hurled

a universe. He sleeps
whose eyelids have not closed before.
His breath (so slight it seems
no breath at all) once ruffled the dark deeps
to sprout a world.
Charmed by dove's voices, the whisper of straw,
he dreams,
hearing no music from his other spheres.
Breath, mouth, ears, eyes
he is curtailed
who overflowed all skies,
all years.
Older than eternity, now he
is new. Now nature to earth as I am, nailed to
my poor planet, caught that I might be free,
blind in my womb to know my darkness ended,
brought to this birth
for me to be new-born,
and for him to see me mended
I must see him torn.

Luci Shaw

Messianic blues

What kind of Saviour?
a soft shoe shuffle
hair never ruffled
chocolate truffle Saviour
a finger in the air
stickers everywhere Saviour
a neat
sweet
petite
graffit-i Saviour

a monopolised
homogenised
before your eyes
compromising Saviour
a cure for your back ache
wrapped in soap flakes
explodes from huge birthday cakes
a Stars on Sunday
have your own way
a dressed in drag
drives a jag
a left wing right wing
centre forward
upside down
wrong way round
3p a pound Saviour
a half day closing
always dozing Saviour
a carpenter from Galilee
who simply said
follow me . . . Saviour.

Stewart Henderson

An arrest

Last night Father Christmas was
        arrested
He was detained by the SPG
for causing a riotous assembly,
        a fracas,
a public disturbance, an etcetera
Also apprehended were several goblins,
numerous creatures with bells
        on their heads

pointed feet and green hair
These characters were later
    identified by the authorities
as probable illegal immigrants
A reindeer was also taken into custody
for driving a sleigh with a bald hoof
The Police State
that Christmas was under close
    surveillance for several minutes
as were his accomplices
The accused were seen in Oxford Street
banging tambourines, lampposts
and sometimes each other
and dancing steps never seen before
Christmas, the Police went on,
was by this time
emerging as the ring leader
He pushed into bus queues
and was seen to entice
disgruntled shoppers dreaming of
    hot baths
jaded bank clerks knee deep in
    mince pies
and innocent children
to partake in the senseless anarchy
A display of this sort by a fat
    red man
who claims he hails from the planet
    of stars
has caused penetrating question
    to be asked in the House
but as usual nobody has come up
    with an answer
Draped, robed and caressed in tinsel
Father Christmas alias Santa Claus
was bundled into the back of a squad car
his cheeks like fire engines glowing
    in the neon evening

The Police confirmed that no
    illegal substances
were found in his possession
however it was noticed
he smelt strongly of snow and wood smoke
When charged Christmas pleaded to an outbreak
of spontaneous joy
Asked if he had anything further
    to add
he chuckled with child like glee
    and said
'Bethlehem, Bethlehem, the joy,
    the joy of Bethlehem.'

Stewart Henderson

Royal baby

Funny the way some kings are born
Amidst lip bitten crowds
    hushed bunting
and big eyed television cameras

The proclamation as Sainsbury
    champagne corks
ricochet off clouds
Video king of a bleak and techno land

The rattling natter of journalists
parrots with press cards
as crimplene ladies with stout
    forearms
and gold wrist watches beam happily,
catalogue angels on rent rebates
And then there was the man with
    pebble glasses and green teeth

One handled grimy tartan shopping bag
full of mallets and bread knives
as the crowd murmured appreciation
     for quick thinking policemen
probably end up as a headline
     somewhere
'Nutter nailed at Royal Rave up'
Funny the way some kings are born
Funny the way some kings are born
three strange visitors on camels
bring seemingly impractical gifts
as the smell of animal dung
seeps and creeps into the sharp
     black night
the breath of God lies kicking
     in straw
whilst outside
the man with pebble glasses and
     green teeth
sniggers to the sheep
'He's a bastard you know'
Funny the way some kings are born

Stewart Henderson

Easter prayer

O God, may we never forget all that you have done for us.
Help us to remember that you sent your Son to die.
And when we think of Christ, when we think of His
death, and of His agony;
We are bewildered by the price you were willing to pay.
For He died to give us: Life in place of death; Hope for
our despair; Joy in place of our frustrations; Light in place
of darkness:
Yet we are frightened by the implications of it all.

For we must confess that we love darkness rather than
Light;
Because the Light exposes our frailty, And demands we
live as beacons in the midst of this world's darkness.
And we love the darkness—and in the darkness we have
betrayed you.

For we love our nice respectable sins;
we love to get our own way;
And we love things to be done our way.
And as for your demands—
The demand of Jesus to 'Come and follow me'.
Well, we'd rather just live our own lives;
we don't want to get involved;
we will live our lives and we'll let the rest live theirs.

If only you had come as a triumphant King,
instead of dying as a criminal,
Then it would have been easy to follow you,
easy to worship you.
And yet our worship would have been false,
Ours would have been a union of fear instead of love.

For it is in your death;
in your death on that cross;
in your agony;
in those great cries from Calvary of mingled love and pain.
That we are united with God—Our Father.

For through your pain—you have changed the world,
through your agony—you have changed us,
through your death—you have united us with yourself.
And through your love—you challenge, demand,
compel us to follow.

And so we ask, that you will enable us to follow you—
The Risen Triumphant Lord.
For the wonder and glory of our existence, is

That you are ALIVE.
Alive for evermore.
Alive and present with us now.

So we praise you—we worship you, and
Ask you to give us the grace to follow you as your
disciples.

In the name of the Living Christ.

Amen.

Jesus is alive

Check this before using and bring up to date if necessary.

Jesus Christ is alive, the Queen is alive, Edward Heath is
alive, Harold Wilson is alive, Margaret Thatcher is alive,
Neil Kinnock is alive, David Steel is alive, David Owen is
alive, *Jesus is alive*, Billy Graham is alive, Cliff Richard is
alive, *Jesus is alive*, Barabbas is dead, *Jesus is alive*, Buddha
is dead, *Jesus is alive*, Confucius is dead, *Jesus is alive*,
Socrates is dead, Alexander the Great is dead, Caesar is
dead, Nero is dead, *Jesus is alive*, Luther is dead, Calvin is
dead, *Jesus is alive*, Napoleon is dead, Wellington is dead,
Bismark is dead, *Jesus is alive*, Karl Marx is dead, Sigmund
Freud is dead, Charles Darwin is dead, *Jesus is alive*,
Winston Churchill is dead, President Kennedy is dead,
John Lennon is dead, Marvin Gaye is dead, Bob Marley is
dead, *Jesus is alive*, Martin Luther King is dead, *Jesus is
alive*, You are living, *Jesus is living.*

Jesus is alive. . . .

adapted by Tony Jasper

One solitary life

Here is a man who was born in an obscure village, the child of a peasant woman. He worked in a carpenter's shop until he was thirty, and then for three years he was an itinerant preacher. He had no credentials but himself. While still a young man, the tide of popular opinion turned against him. His friends—the twelve men who had learned so much from him and had promised him their enduring loyalty—ran away, and left him. He went through a mockery of a trial; he was nailed upon a cross between two thieves; when he was dead, he was taken down and laid in a borrowed grave through the pity of a friend. Yet I am well within the mark when I say that all the armies that ever marched, and all the parliaments that ever sat, and all the kings that ever reigned, put together, have not affected the life of man upon the earth as has this one solitary life.

PART FIVE

Words of Liberation

**Human liberation
Pray to the Lord
God's big time has begun
Commitment—real risk**

Notes on Part Five extracts

Human liberation. Once the introduction has been said on a leader/people responsive basis verses can be taken by individuals or groups. This piece is full of vitality and energy. Establish a rhythm and keep pushing the lines along fairly rapidly. Afterwards have someone talk about the way their particular Christian community is learning to live the 'life' in difficult times and situations.

Commitment—real risk. Ask the gathering to join hands. Alternatively, ask people to disperse around the church and then, somewhat in party fashion, clap and then link hands with those near to them. By this latter means, people will link with those they rarely speak with or sit next to. They will then be more aware that their commitment is not just to those friends they usually sit with but to others. 'Commitment' is not intended as a pleasant exercise or simply a different way to bring the worship service to a close. As each line is said it might prove useful to have someone add a further thought. If the line 'to challenge evil' is read then the 'evil' might be tangibly seen as apartheid. Should something have happened around the time of the gathering then this event relating to apartheid might be described.

Human liberation

A time for coming together

Leader: We have come here to celebrate 'Life'!

People: Yes! We are celebrating in spite of the conditions we live under—war, racism, poverty, greed, sexism, exploitation, repression, guilt and loneliness.

Leader: We have come here to share an experience of 'Life' together.

People: Yes! We have come together and accept our differences.

Leader: We have come here to decide to live.

People: Yes! Yes! Living is a righteous experience.

Leader: Life is you and me and everyone else.
Life is always growing, always reaching.
Life is having roots in the past,
  being nourished by the present,
  budding through to the new.
Life comes in all colours—all beautiful!

Life is great.
Life is loving—and being loved.
Life is free to be who we're meant to be.
Life is enough food to eat.
Life is work you're proud to do.

Life is clothing to wear when you need it.
Life is health care for everybody who needs it.
Life is free child care for the mamas who need it.

Life is the exciting unknown. Life is hope!
Life is spontaneity.
Life is being where you have to be when it's
  happening.
Life is surviving even though the odds are
  against you.

Life is saying Hey Man! Hey Woman! 'cause
    you're you.
Life is making mistakes, admitting them, and
    movin' on!
Life is anger and telling it like it is.
Life is laughter and joy.

Life is confrontation and letting be.
Life is sadness and loneliness.
Life is being who you are:
Life is the children.

Life is feeding the hungry,
    clothing the naked,
    freeing the prisoners.
Life is freedom for all people—
    in the ghettos,
    in the barrios,
    in the reservations—No More Wounded Knees!
    in the prisons of people's minds.
Life is being heard and hearing others.
Life is knowing you are somebody.

Life is being concerned for people,
    not because it's good politics, nor good
        business;
    not because it's good religion, nor good
        strategy,
    not because it's good seduction,
    but because you really care for someone.
Life is openness,
Life is not just words in a Book,
    but flesh, and body, action, and revolution!

Rev A. Cecil Williams

Pray to the Lord

Let us break the bread the Lord has given us.
    Let all who are hungry join us and eat.
Let all who are thirsty come in and celebrate with us.
    This year there are still men and women in slavery.
    Next year may all men and women be free!
Sing to the Lord
Let us break bread together with the Lord!
Let us break bread together with the Lord!
As we travel through this land
with our brothers and sisters hand-in-hand
O Lord fill our livin' with your life!

God's big time has begun

    Now the times are filled full
    Now is the day of wholeness
    Now God's place is within humanity
    Now the time of liberation has arrived
    Now is the celebration of the Kingdom

Commitment—real risk

Let us commit ourselves, as far as we can, to live by the
things we have seen, and known, in the power of Jesus.

We commit ourselves:
    to hold to the truth as it is in Jesus,
    to support each other in good and ill,

to challenge evil with the power of love,
to offer the Kingdom in political and economic witness,
to work for the new community of humanity,
and to risk ourselves in a lifestyle of sharing.

The Grace of the Lord Jesus be always with us.

Amen

PART SIX

Words of Meditation

Three meditations
Christ our Light!
Our peace
Always there

Notes on Part Six extracts

Before worship/prayer or for a time of reflection, getting ready for a set appointment with God:

Sit quietly, eyes cast down or closed, reflecting on the possibilities of this gathering of Christian lovers of peace, deepening your own personal hopes for today, your thankfulness that so many share your ideals and are one with you.

Slow down your restless mind for a time. Breathe very slowly, deliberately, consciously. . . . Each breath is God's gift of life to you. It comes to you as regularly as His graces and blessings. He says 'Be still and see that I am God.' Repeat these words silently in your heart . . . savour their meaning. Consider how close He is to you at this moment. You are never truly alone for He abides in your heart, your constant companion. Try to relax and enjoy this truth. He alone is your security, the foundations of your life.

Place all your hopes and dreams in His hands for this important day in your life. Let His peace rejoice and nourish your spirit. Praise Him with inner silence. Experience in this stillness a new sense of timelessness, wonder and awe in His presence. Turn to the Lord with your concerns and ask Him to direct this day for the good of all and the advancement of peace.

Jesus, may we be more attentive to Your voice calling us to peace not war, love not hate, to forgive not to retaliate, to listen and try to understand, not to shout and close our minds and hearts. Give us the strength to drop our defences and do away with our weapons and to encircle our brothers and sisters all over God's world in understanding love.

Three meditations

words and visuals
The left hand text suggests the visual content of slides you may select to illustrate the words in the right hand column. Read the words slowly, while the appropriate slide is shown.

One

CROWDED STREET

People everywhere
It's crushed
hot
I feel like screaming
What's all the fuss
A carpenter stands up to read the lesson
And everyone goes wild
I don't get it.

TIRED, WORRIED
LOOKING
INDIVIDUALS
IN THE CROWD

People everywhere
It's crushed
It's uncomfortable
I feel like screaming
It's such a scramble
I don't get it.

TUBE TRAIN

On and off the Circle Line

OFFICE

In and out the filing cabinet
On and off the phone
I don't get it.

HOUSEWIFE

In and out the kitchen
Up and down the stairs
Round and round this market
I don't get it.

MEN AND WOMEN TOGETHER	Jesus stood up amongst them and read 'The spirit of the Lord' is upon me because he has anointed me to preach good news to the poor
REPEAT SLIDE OF TIRED INDIVIDUALS IN CROWD	Freedom for prisoners Sight for the blind Release for the oppressed

Two

CITY SCENE AT NIGHT	I love you I hate you Your life Vitality Colour Excitement draws me and then disappoints me
HIGH-RISE CONCRETE JUNGLE	I love you and hate you your splendour history and majesty fills me with wonder but then after a while stifles me
VIEW OF JERUSALEM	And Jesus looked over the city and sighed O Jerusalem, Jerusalem How I would love to gather you under my wings, like a hen gathers her chicks But you would not

Three

A WASTELAND, RUBBISH TIP OR A DERELICT BUILDING

In the rubbish tip
Outside the City
There is resurrection

In the wreckage
of thrown-away
forgotten
relationships
there can be resurrection

In the disfigured
scarred
places
there can be resurrection

In the confusion
of crowds
of chaos
There can be resurrection

In darkness
and loneliness
There can be resurrection

Blessed is He who comes
in the name of God
Hosanna, Hosanna

Christt our Light!

This could be done after a candle-making project or just by itself. Just place a candle in the middle of the room, but don't light it. Start off in darkness; let everyone get used to it and the giggles die down. Mention a few things: isolation, fear, insecurity, etc. Somebody reads John 1:1–5 to one side by candlelight, then lights the candle in the centre (or possibly each person's candle?). Allow a moment's reflection. Then:

Leader: At the beginning
Everyone: Christ our Light
Leader: In the Scriptures
Everyone: Christ our Light
Leader: Through history
Everyone: Christ our Light
Leader: In the present
Everyone: Christ our Light.

End by saying the following words a couple of times to the tune of Frère Jacques—*sing in a round if you're brave!*

> Christ our Light,
> Christ our Light
> Light our lives.
> Light our lives.
> We'll be a light to others.
> We'll be a light to others.
> Light our lives,
> Light our lives.

John Bell

Our peace

This is a suggestion for a simple meditation on the theme of peace, using selected verses from the NIV Bible. It is no more than an outline; therefore those who use it should add their own choice of prayers, choruses/hymns and other material.

Peace is something we experience. As you meet with others and relax in God's presence, remember how much He cares for you and rejoice in the promise that nothing can separate us from His love.

The origin of our peace

'. . . the Lord blesses his people with peace'.

Psalm 29:11

'For God is not a God of disorder but of peace'

1 Corinthians 14:33

What Christ has done for us

'Praise be to the Lord, the God of Israel, because he has come and has redeemed his people . . . to guide our feet into the path of peace'

(Zechariah's song) Luke 1:68, 79

'Peace I leave with you; my peace I give you'

John 14:27

'I have told you these things, so that in me you may have peace. In this world you will have trouble. But take heart! I have overcome the world'

John 16:33

Being at peace with yourself and with others

'. . . You will know the truth, and the truth will set you free'

John 8:32

'Live in peace with each other'

1 Thessalonians 5:13

'Peacemakers who sow in peace raise a harvest of righteousness'

James 3:18

Peace is good for you!

'A heart at peace gives life to the body . . .'

Proverbs 14:30

'Better a dry crust with peace and quiet than a house full of
feasting, with strife'

Proverbs 17:1

'. . . the fruit of the Spirit is love, joy, peace . . .'

Galatians 5:22

Finally . . .

'Do not fret because of evil men or be envious of those who
do wrong; . . . Trust in the Lord and do good; . . . there is a
future for the man of peace'

Psalm 37:1, 3 and 37

S. W. Andrew

Always there

You wait for us
until we are open to you.
We wait for your word
to make us receptive.
Attune us to your voice,
to your silence,
speak and bring your son to us—
Jesus, the word of your peace
Your word is near,
O Lord our God,

your grace is near.
Come to us, then,
with mildness and power.
Do not let us be dear to you,
but make us receptive and open
to Jesus Christ your son,
who will come to look for us and save us
today and every day
for ever and ever.

You, God, arouse faith in our hearts,
whoever we are.
You know and accept all your people,
whatever their thoughts are of you.
Speak to the world, then, your word,
come with your heaven among us,
give to good and to bad people your sun,
for ever and ever.

Grant us, O Lord,
a sign of life,
show us, O God,
how much we mean to you.
Come into our world
with your word of creation
Make us fit to receive you,
and grant us your peace.

Sow freely, Lord God,
the seed of your word over the world.
May it fall in good soil in us
and may it be heard
wherever people live.

Do not turn from us, God,
and do not avoid us

now that we are looking
for words to pray to you.
For if we call you God
and speak your name
we do so because you have promised
that you will not be far from all
who call upon you.

Huub Oosterhuis   6-3

PART SEVEN

Words of Life

He makes things explode!
How can I know the other person's pain?
Fears
Coping with the undesirable
A prayer from Ravensbruck Concentration Camp
Dejection
At the start of a difficult day
Opposites can be best
The shrinkage back
Final question
Christ and Thomas
Opening responses
He is always present and waiting
Sisters and brothers, arise
All things for declaring in His presence
Closing responses
We have a gospel to proclaim
The world from African eyes
The secular and sacred are incompatible
Here am I
Why travel so far?
Hands of Jesus
We are not alone
Just as we are—thankfully
People can be people

Notes on Part Seven extracts

Some of the readings in this section express confusion and doubt, conditions adequately known and understood only by the sufferer. However, the use of case study, illustration from a printed source, even powerful word imagery, can help achieve a greater realism before these prayers are said. If possible take time to listen to someone who has experienced the states of mind expressed in these readings. *Fears* will probably find immediate recognition with the gathering, although people may be unwilling to reveal their insecurities—especially if theirs is an underlying assumption that Christians should operate on a mysterious high. Different voices can be used for 'Fears'. In a fairly mature group setting someone might later ask, 'What makes us afraid?'

A prayer from Ravensbruck Concentration Camp. This prayer can be used when the theme of the worship is peace or reconciliation. Recall how many have suffered and are still suffering because of man's inhumanity to man.

At the start of a difficult day. This might be followed by a number of people describing a day in their life when God felt absent and of how on reflection they have sensed His presence was there.

Opposites can be best. This prayer can be broadened to include the experiences of the people gathered. Ask the congregation for similar examples in their lives.

The shrinkage back will not be an easy poem for some Christian circles which have relegated the sensuous but it should lead to a consideration of this theme.

He is always present and waiting. This needs two readers, a leader and the voice of Christ. Some of the responses are designed to be said by all the people present. Remember to distribute copies to the gathering beforehand. Some direction/explanation will be necessary at the beginning of the service so people feel comfortable joining in. It may be helpful to have one person to lead the congregational response.

Sisters and brothers, arise. The gathering should stand for this reading which should be spoken out in ringing tones. *Hands of Jesus* and *We are not alone* are intended to be said by all.

Take time can be effectively read by two voices. For example, Reader 1 makes the statement, 'Take time to think', and Reader 2 follows with 'It is the source of power'. The final line can be read by both voices together after a dramatic pause.

Once. This can be used to lead into a discussion on people and events that have altered our perceptions and feelings.

The dance of the Holy Trinity. This obviously lends itself to interpretative dance. Music for dance can be found in Section 8 at the back of the book, together with a list of several excellent books on this subject.

He makes things explode!

It will be a river
my small voice in you
which now trails weakly like a
stream among boulders

it will burn bright
the light which glows so strong
so long, then flickers
wildly, blows unsteadily

Clowns now, you will be dancers
at my throne. Do you not see it
all fears gone
you will wear glory like a gown

For now be foolish, clumsy
stumble, fall,
All shall be well
and being unwhole is part of travelling.

Let me hear your heart sing
be my clown
and it will be a river
my small truth in you.

(Based on 2 Corinthians 4:17)
Jill Harris

How can I know the other person's pain?

A prayer

Almighty God,
I, who have never known what it means not to have the things I desire, need to *feel* the poverty and hunger and despair among my fellow men and women.
I, who have felt nothing but the surge of youthful vitality in my body, need to *understand* what it means to be ill and unable to care for myself.
I, who have never stood alone in the crowd as odd or unacceptable, need to *sense* what it means to be judged and rejected by the colour of my skin.
I, who have never experienced the desperation of a dependence on drug or drink, need to *realise* the hell of an addiction I cannot escape.
I, who have never really suffered or sacrificed or died, pray that I may become painfully aware of my brother's great need and that I may *ache* until I have reached out with honest help.

Kay Lorans Hancock

Fears

We are afraid
afraid of people,
of the dark,
of evil,
of illness,
of death.

We are afraid of insects that bring disease,
of snakes,

of attack from wild animals,
of accidents.

We fear many things,
but we don't like to admit it to anyone.
We let our friends think we are brave,
but deep down we are afraid.

We are afraid of being scorned,
and laughed at by other students,
of being despised for doing right.

We fear the future;
leaving school to begin work,
to take responsibility.
We fear the final exams,
failure,
the prospect of unemployment
and poverty.

We are afraid of being sent home
with a bad report at the end of term;
afraid of being sent to the head
for some misdeed.
We are afraid of punishment,
of suspension,
of being sent home from school.

We are afraid of answering a question in class;
afraid of looking foolish before others.

We are afraid of fire.
We are scared at the slightest sound
we hear in the night,
afraid that thieves may break in
and attack us.

We are afraid of the fate
that may face us in the course of a day;
that sad news may come in the form of a letter,
or a phone call,
or a visit.

We are afraid when problems face our country
and the world.
We are afraid of war
of tribal conflicts,
of those nations who have atomic weapons,
of flood and earthquakes;
of anything which might destroy our homes
and bring death to innocent people.

'I am afraid to accept Jesus Christ,
and to join Christian meetings;
I am afraid that people
will start watching me
and asking questions.

I fear hypocrisy and fanaticism
among Christian students.
I fear the second coming of our Lord;
I fear his judgement.

Some girls of Limuru Girls' School, Kenya penned these thoughts. Several of the allusions have an African reference and these (as of course other thoughts) can be rephrased to suit local expression. Gathered and edited by Maureen Edwards.

Coping with the undesirable

O God, I get awfully tired of static.
I am fed up with the flak that comes my way
    from those I am trying to serve.
It seems that they suspect or misinterpret
    or question my motives or authority
    in respect to everything I do or say.
I think people enjoy putting me down.
I just can't get them off my back.

Do I have to perpetually live
    with this sort of thing, O Lord?
What about this joy that is promised to those
    who are Your servants and ministers?

Forgive me my unworthy thoughts, O Lord.
Overlook my vicious complaints,
    and so fill my heart with Your love
    that I will respond in love
    even toward those who cannot love me.
Enable me, O Lord, to find my joy in You
    and to reflect that joy to the unresponsive,
    reactionary, disagreeable people
    who do not like me very much.

Leslie F. Brandt's Modern Reading of the Psalms

A prayer
from Ravensbruck Concentration Camp

O Lord,
remember not only the men and women of good will,
but those of ill will.
But do not remember all the suffering
they have inflicted upon us;
remember the fruits we have bought
thanks to this suffering—
our comradeship, our loyalty, our humility, our courage,
      our generosity, the greatness of heart
which has grown out of all this;
and when they come to the judgement,
let all the fruits which we have borne
be their forgiveness.

(Found on a piece of wrapping paper beside the body of a dead child at Ravensbruck Concentration Camp.)

Dejection

Please welcom this lump of dejection,
That is me, Father.
I can't lift up my head,
I can't start to look for you,
But please take me as I am,
And help me through the dark.
I can't offer you energy or enthusiasm,
I can't offer you love or worship,
I can only offer me,
Drawn in and hurting,
Please hold me gently, Lord—Amen.

At the start of a difficult day

Life gets tedious.

Today
is far too much like
yesterday
and the day before yesterday,
and
the day before that.
I don't want to get on with the business of living
today.

I know what jobs I've got to do
and I don't want to do them.
I know what people I've got to meet
and I don't want to meet them.
I know the places I've got to go,
and I don't want to go there.

As I look at them
the tiniest duties of the day
become enormous.
Today
I feel beaten before I start.
Did you ever feel like this,
Jesus?
That's funny!
As soon as I ask the question
something is different.
There's a shift in the perspective
of what is visible
as I look at
today.

For now I see that
today
contains Christ.

He has become a part of this terrible day.
And the day is not so terrible.
He has gone before.
Already he is present in the midst of everything
that makes it dreary—
the dreariness begins to disappear.
It's as if the sun is beginning to shine.

Dick Williams

Opposites can be best

I asked God for strength, that I might achieve,
I was made weak, that I might learn humbly to obey.
I asked for health, that I might do greater things,
I was given infirmity, that I might do better things.
I asked for riches, that I might be happy,
I was given poverty, that I might be wise.
I asked for power, that I might have the praise of men,
I was given weakness, that I might feel the need of God.
I asked for all things, that I might enjoy life,
I was given life, that I might enjoy all things.
I got nothing that I asked for—
but everything I had hoped for.
Almost despite myself, my
unspoken prayers were answered.
I am, among all men,
    most richly blessed.

Anonymous Confederate soldier

The shrinkage back

Leant at the glass
you touch your face.

Your skin is changeable,
it suffers with the cold,
the winter it sloughs off;
yet it is cared for both

by you with water
and by my bare hands.
Skins meet against the elements
and wear each other down,
the shrinkage back
to what our skins contain;

our bodies, changeable,
that will be changed.

Senses more deft than touch
feel for our glorious bodies

Paul Hyland

Paul Hyland is one of Britain's most promising poets. This poem is taken from his excellent collection **The Stubborn Forest***.*

Final question

How can you pass a river
without wanting to plunge and swim?
or a tree with low-limbed branches
and not swing up within?

Some people don't want to climb hills;
how come? Fancy passing a door
without peering in—
O sorry!
Can you see a puzzle
without trying to solve it?
or a waggling dog
without fondling its ears?
meet a friend and not want to hug them?
hear music and not wish to dance?
see a ditch and not jump it?
a flower and not smell it?
a fire and not poke it?
sense God and not love?

Graham Claydon

Christ and Thomas

All of my dismay came falling out of me.

Nothing happened.
None of the things
you think he'd say
if only he would come.

I should have said
—excuse me, but
you don't understand.

Some of us are blind
though we have eyes,
are deaf, not having your
heaven-scanning ears,
your easy holy spirit
photosynthesis
(pity us) are walled about
with flesh.

I should have hung
upon his shoulders
shrieking, eyes aflame,
done all the things
you think you'd do
if only he would come.

Instead of which
I simply stared
dumbly appalled
my dismay falling
to the silent ground

And he, merely
looked at me coolly
through blue eyes,
touched my hand and said
I was one of the lucky ones,
others would
have a much harder time.

After which one might think
one would never doubt again.

Jill Harris

Opening responses

One

Leader: In the beginning, when it was very dark, God said, 'Let there be Light'

Response: *And there was Light* (The sign of the light—a lighted candle is placed centrally.)

Leader: In the beginning, when it was very quiet, The Word was with God.

Response: *And what God was, the Word was.* (The sign of the Word—an open Bible is placed centrally.)

Leader: When the time was right, God sent His Son.

Response: *He came among us. He was one of us.* (The sign of the Son—a cross—is placed centrally.)

Two

Leader: Let us take off our shoes

Response: *For the ground we stand on is holy.*

Leader: Let us bend down

Response: *For the door to the Kingdom is low.*

Leader: Let us speak quietly

Response: *For the ear of the Almighty is never deaf.*

Leader: Let us expect much

Response: *For the King of Kings has promises to keep.*

John Bell

He is always present and waiting

Leader: When the lights are on
    And the house is full
    And the laughter is easy
    And all is well
        Christ: Behold I stand at the door and knock.
Leader: When the lights are low
    And the house is still
    And the talk is intense
    And the air is full of wondering
        Christ: Behold I stand at the door and knock.
Leader: When the lights are off
    And the house is sad
    And the voice is troubled
    And nothing seems right
        Christ: Behold I stand at the door and knock.
Leader: And tonight
    Always tonight
    As if there were no other people
                no other house
                no other door
        Christ: Behold I stand at the door and knock.
Leader: Come Lord Jesus, be our guest
    Stay with us for day is ending
    Bring to our house your poverty
All: *For then we shall be rich*
Leader: Bring to our house your pain
All: *That sharing it we may also share your joy*
Leader: Bring to our house your understanding of us
All: *That we may be freed to learn more of you*
Leader: Bring to our house all those
    Who hurry or hirple behind you
All: *That we may meet you as Saviour of all*
Leader: Bring to our house your Holy Spirit
All: *That this may be a cradle of love*
Leader: With friend, with stranger,
    With neighbour, with well-known ones,

Be among us tonight.

All: *For the doors of our house, we open
and the doors of our heart we leave ajar.*

John Bell

Sisters and brothers, arise

Sisters and brothers, arise.
Arise and lift your hearts
Arise and lift your eyes
Arise and lift your voices.

The living God,
The living, moving Spirit of God
has called us together—
in witness
in celebration
in struggle.

Reach out toward each other,
Our God reaches out toward us!
Let us worship God!

Elizabeth Rice

All things for declaring in His presence

If you love to weep, weep! Empty your tensions,
frustrations, in the house of God. Weep and say 'Amen'.
Weep and say, 'Hallelujah', weep and say, 'Praise the
Lord'. Mix sorrow with joy; mix anxiety with hope.
Weep and walk on; weep and fight; weep and struggle:
weep and forget about the past, lest you, like Lot's wife,
be turned into a pillar of salt. Weep, and let there be
daylight in your life. Weep, and let there be sunshine.

Louis Chase

Closing responses

One

Leader: Look at your hands
       See the touch and the tenderness
Response: *God's own for the world*
Leader: Look at your feet
       See the path and direction
Response: *God's own for the world*
Leader: Look at your heart
       See the fire and the love
Response: *God's own for the world*
Leader: Look at the cross
       See God's Son and our Saviour
Response: *God's own for the world*
Leader: This is God's world
Response: *And we will serve Him in it*
Leader: May God bless you, may He keep you for ever
       in His care. And lead your lives with love.
Response: *Amen.*

Two

Leader: The cross
Response: *We shall take it*
Leader: The bread
Response: *We shall break it*
Leader: The pain
Response: *We shall bear it*
Leader: The joy
Response: *We shall share it*
Leader: The Gospel
Response: *We shall live it*
Leader: The love
Response: *We shall give it*
Leader: The light
Response: *We shall cherish it*
Leader: The darkness
Response: *God shall perish it*

John Bell

We have a gospel to proclaim

We have a gospel to proclaim
but instead we dilute it to taste
coat it with sugar
and give it away
with exciting free gifts,
presenting it
in a choice of appetising flavours.
We have a gospel to proclaim
but instead we speak
of mile-wide toothpaste smiles,
bingo bonanzas
and angels playing golden harps
on fluffy marshmallow clouds.

The gospel which we proclaim
does not mention nasty things
like persecution or pain
torture or tears.
We have no time
for sweat, blood,
crosses or rusty nails.
We want pre-packaged
easy to swallow faith
neatly turned out
in Sunday best.
We have a gospel to proclaim
but we have lost something
in the translation.

Mark Reaney

The world from African eyes
From the beginning You have guided Africa

Darkly and dimly have we known
That you are near and everywhere.
We see you in lightning and the trees,
We hear you in thunder and waterfalls,
We feel your presence in the prayer and the dance.
With the old men under the tree,
The young men in their age group,
Women in the market place.
In full have you participated,
Darkly and dimly have we known this.
Our pale brothers from over the seas came,
With the book of life they proclaimed the good news.
This is Him, we have felt His presence.
This is Him, we have heard in the council.
Though darkly and dimly this was Him!

For joy we shouted, this is Him!
No, said our brothers,
This was not Him.
In darkness have you been sitting:
Listen to the word or you perish.
Away from the market place,
Away from the party and the council.
Away from the trade union.
Away, away! Away, brothers away.
Away, away from the world.

Bethel A. Kiplagat

The secular and sacred are incompatible

Feverishly we clung together in prayer,
In fellowship groups we confessed our sins
And condemned the world.
Together we huddled in the church
To shut away the anguish of the freedom fighters,
The agonies of the politicians,
The conflict of the racial situation.
From our painted church window
We see shadows of men dashing to and fro.
We hear the cry of the mother
Deprived of her husband.
No, we cannot stand it any longer.
Dimly but clearly we hear Him cry.
A few heard the voice, stood and left the church.
The door of the church was shut behind them,
And there with Him they joined the conflict.

Bethel A. Kiplagat

Here am I

This is my flesh.
I give it to you.
These are my thoughts,
and this is my work.
Here are my faults.
Here is the fear
I discuss with myself.
Here are my good jokes,
here are my bad ones.
The flesh is falling apart,
it will have to do.
The thoughts are uncontrollable
some of them hate each other.

Here is my sweat,
and my decay,
the face only mirrors see.
This is my love
and my lack of love.
Here is my laughter.
Here are the years.
Here am I.

Steve Turner

Why travel so far?

To which temple are you going?
Where do you find your God?
Which goods do you worship, O man?

Sitting on the shoulders of men
Are you carried to their temple:
   Pillars of the bones
   Walls of the muscles
   Doors of sensation
Roof of the gold-thirsty mind?
   Listen with hearing ears
   Deeper than skin and eyes
   Listen to the song that God speaks:
      'Go, ease the foot of the weary,
      Soothe the wounds of those who weep from the heart,
      Be one who brings happiness,
      Fill with joy the face of the poor.'
         He gives you the palm branch, he is God;
         Sing with him the psalm of victory.
         God lives in your heart—
         Why travel so far to look for him?
            'Be a man who brings help,
            Succour the weak and poverty stricken.

*The original poem was written in Nepali and this is an
adaptation of the person's own English translation. The writer
is a Christian convert from the Hindu religion.*

Hands of Jesus

A blessing

All: *Hands of Jesus, bless us; feet of Jesus, lead us; arms of Jesus, uphold us; heart of Jesus, burn in us. Presence of Jesus, be in our neighbour.*

Leader: Go in peace to serve the Lord.

All: *May we live and work to His praise and glory.*

We are not alone

We are not alone; we live in God's world.

We believe in God
who has created and is creating;
who has come in Jesus to reconcile
and make new.

We trust God
who calls us to be the church;
to love and serve others;
to seek justice and resist evil;
to proclaim Jesus, crucified and risen,
our judge and our hope.

In life, in death, in life beyond death,
God is with us.
We are not alone.

Thanks be to God.

Just as we are—thankfully

In the presence of the Lord Jesus Christ, we need no masks:
we are known
and loved;
no hiding of ourselves is possible or necessary.

People can be people

*A litany based on 1 John 4, especially 1 John 4:12, 20, 21.
Two readers are needed. An imaginative person could develop
some interpretative movements so that the reading could be
acted out by a group of people as well as read. Alternatively one
half of the gathering could be reader 2 and the other, reader 2.*

Reader 1:   I have seen—
a boy named Gene,
a girl named Lillian,
an old man beside a broken down car,
a child crying because he is lost,
a child running effortlessly and deliriously
    happy
I have seen people.
I have seen Christ.

Reader 2:   Today I have seen—
(*the reader makes his/her own observations as
to how he/she has seen Christ reflected in the
lives of people*)*
I have seen people.
I have seen Christ.

Reader 1:   People are hell, but they're heaven too.

Reader 2:   People hate

Reader 1:   People care

Reader 2:   People love

---

* other people could add their thoughts.

Reader 1:	People need people
Reader 2:	People need love
Reader 1:	The love of God
Reader 2:	the love of each other
Reader 1:	People need people. People need friends, lovers, neighbours. People need to be needed.
Readers 1 & 2:	You need to be needed and you need to be loved.
Reader 2:	Why all the talk about people? Such a distant word. You're here. I'm here. We're people. Let's talk about us.
Reader 1:	A wall is tumbling. The wall of distance is coming down, when you speak about *us*. We always have the walls up. Walls to keep people out. Walls to keep people from getting too close.
Reader 2:	We live and act that way. We use words to keep people away. Yet we keep waiting for the walls to crack and crumble. We keep waiting to open and live.
Reader 1:	People need people. People need love.
Reader 2:	And the courage to reach out. To reach out and ask, to reach out and give.
Reader 1:	It's frightening, it's scary, but necessary too. To reach out to another person, whether to ask for help or to give some aid, means taking the chance of being turned away.
Reader 2: (*Pause*)	Rejected. Despised. Terribly lonely.
Reader 2:	Always closer than we want, always closer than we think.
Reader 1:	It may be that some of us, in this crowd, in our group, are alone. Who is he, who is she? Where? The walls keep us out.
Reader 2:	(**Shout** *it out, as if in agony*) How do you break free? Tear down the walls, turn on the people?

Reader 1:	How? By reaching out, by taking the chance, and letting it be known who you are and how you feel. By making the break with the world of self-pretence.

The practice

Reader 2:	We offer you that chance now, of making the break, of cracking the wall. Go to one person in this gathering—someone you've not met—take his/her hands, look him in the eye, ask this question, 'I'd like to know how you feel about life at the moment'. Keep hold of both hands until after our closing prayer.

The prayer

Reader 1 offers this prayer, making it a prayer of confession which speaks to God about how well we have succeeded in our honesty. It should reflect our feelings about our experience.
A song sung by all should follow.

Note: do not be too disturbed if this experience is not as good as you would like. The first attempts at group honesty are usually partially successful and no more, filled with nervous laughter and side comments.

Obviously the 'practice' element may not be useful in a general service and may be more suited to a weekend gathering when people have time to further links.

Knocking

A: And sometimes the knock is very loud
B: proud
A: arrogant
B: imperious
A: knock, knock, knock
B: hurry up there!
A: open this door!
B: keeping me waiting!
A: don't you know who I am!
B: come on, come on
A: knock, knock, knock
B: ah! and about time too

A: and sometimes the knock is quite different
B: quiet
A: but not timid
B: gentle
A: but not afraid
B: behold I stand at the door and knock
A: courteous
B: but not a mere formality
A: waiting
B: but not impatient
A: firm
B: but not aggressive
A: a sort of signal
B: but many do not seem to recognise it
A: but those who do recognise it, open the door
B: and He comes in
A: and they eat together
B: and what a meal!
A: happy are those who open the door.
B: and what about those who do not open?
A: He still stands there knocking . . . knocking . . .

John Horner

Ever faithful, ever true

He was a faithful volunteer
As everyone knew
And respected.

God
He made us feel guilty.

He was living proof
That you ask busy people
To do things
As he spent his energy
Leading drives
Heading committees
Planning programmes
Singing in the choir
Cleaning or painting
At Saturday work parties
Spending himself
In the *good* work
Of the Lord
While the rest of us
Were slothful
Spending Saturdays with
Our children
Wives and friends
Relaxing
Laughing
Feeling occasionally
Guilty because
We seldom volunteered.
We gave him a token
Of our appreciation
For all his years
Of *superservice*.

His wife never smiled

His children
Were all grown.
The applause
Never drowned
The loneliness . . .
Of the supervolunteer.

Conrad Weiser

You call that living?

One day, the Good Lord was doing some judging, and
He had three people in front of him. One had died at a
hundred, one at fifty, and one at twenty.

The Lord turned to the hundred year old man, and
said, 'What did you do with your life James?'

The man answered, 'Lord, I worked hard on the
mission field, I banned slavery in the country I worked
in. You used me to bring many people to know and love
You, I have had a wonderful life, it is a joy to give it
back to You. Thank You for everything.'

And the Good Lord smiled.

Then He turned to the man who had died aged fifty.
'Ali, tell me about your life,' He said.

'Lord,' said Ali, 'I have worked hard as a doctor. I
loved every minute of serving You, and it was wonderful
to show Your love to the people around me, and to bring
them Your healing. Thank You.'

And the Good Lord smiled at Ali too.

Then He turned to the young woman who had died at
the age of twenty.

'Tell me about your life Mary.'

Mary was all shaky and did not look up. 'Well, Lord, I
always knew I would die young, I've always been ill and

I couldn't really do anything. You gave me a rotten life, and here it is coming back to You.'

The Good Lord just looked at Mary. 'What do you mean *couldn't* do anything? How did you spend the twenty years I gave you?'

'You call that *living*?' answered Mary crossly. 'Endless operations, endless pain, knowing you're going to die anyway? Parents who just don't understand? What *could* I have done. It's all very well for these two here, they had it all going for them, didn't they?'

The Good Lord stayed silent. Then the girl mumbled, 'Well, I suppose I needn't have been so short with Mum and Dad always, it can't have been easy for them either . . . and I could have answered people's letters, and maybe tried to cheer them up a bit too. I resented their health. I suppose there was quite a bit I could have done.' Then she looked up accusingly at God. 'Why do You always ask so much of people who have nothing, anyway?'

Then the Good Lord turned to an emaciated little child who had only just arrived in Heaven. 'Welcome, child,' He said taking her into His lap. 'This child had nothing,' He said, 'and she gave her last food to her brother.'

Beth Webb

Always and forever

O Lord, we thank you for those
who chose the way of your Son,
our brother Jesus Christ.
In the midst of trial, they held out hope;
in the midst of hatred, they kindled love;
in the midst of persecutions they witnessed to your power;
in the midst of despair they clung to your promise.

For your love and faithfulness
we will at all times praise your name

O Lord, we thank you for the truth they learned and passed
    on to us:
that it is by giving that we shall receive;
it is by becoming weak that we shall be strong;
it is by loving others that we shall be loved;
it is by offering ourselves that the kingdom will unfold;
it is by dying that we shall inherit life everlasting.
Lord, give us courage to follow your way of life.

For your love and faithfulness
we will at all times praise your name.

Quotation and Prayer, WCC, Vancouver

Take time

Take time to think—
it is the source of power.
Take time to read—
it is the foundation of wisdom.

Take time to play—
it is the secret of staying young.

Take time to be quiet—
it is the opportunity to seek God.

Take time to be aware—
it is the opportunity to help others.
Take time to love and be loved—
it is God's greatest gift.

Take time to laugh—
it is the music of the soul.
Take time to be friendly—
it is the road to happiness.

Take time to dream—
it is what the future is made of.
Take time to pray—
it is the greatest power on earth.

'There is a time for everything.'

Ecclesiastes 3

Once

The final whistle blew.
The crowd moved slowly
From the brightly lit arena,
From the temple where they worshipped weekly,
Out to the grimy streets and terraced houses
Of their town.

They grumbled.
For the great, the mighty Rovers

Had been vanquished
(By a Third Division team)
And to some the placard reading
'End of world at hand'
Was true.

Their world embraced their home, their work,
    their beer,
And little else save football.
Strikes and babies, deaths and weddings,
Goals, Cup Finals, holidays,
Just these to vary weeks of non-existence.

Once I was one of them.
Their town was mine,
I lived for Saturdays and soccer,
And I nearly went their way.

A shabby man made all the difference
Standing with a sandwich board
Which said,
'The end of the world is at hand.'

I looked; I read it; and I thought.
I wondered how much I would mind if it were true.
Not much; no not at all; I'd like it.
Peace for evermore.

Then I knew what I should do,
I almost ran.
The river, yes, of course,
Dank and sluggish,
Bricks to weigh me down.

Who'll miss me?
No one, Ma is dead
And Dad is always drunk.
I should've thought of it before,
A lovely dreamless sleep.

I hurried down the dirty, indistinguishable
streets
And just before the bridge
I crammed the bricks in my pockets
And ran on.

No one cares—
Just one long sleep—
No work—
No worries—
Sweet oblivion.
Hurry! Hurry!

She smiled at me, that sad old lady
And I smiled back
Only already I was smiling,
I had smiled first
But I'd hardly seen her.

I had been smiling.
Why? What was funny?
Nothing was funny
I had just been very happy.
Happy? . . . Happy . . .

Yes . . . Yes, of course I was
Not because of the bricks and the river
But because I had a purpose.
I was going somewhere for a change
Instead of drifting semi-conscious to the grave.

The dance of the Holy Trinity

(*Introductory music*)

Chorus   I am God the Lord
(3 voices)   Father, Son and Spirit
           God, the Three in One
           God whose name is Love

(*music—Theme 1*)

Father   I am God the Father
           Source of all beginning
           Centre of all life
           Well of light and love

           And it is my pleasure
           That all things should prosper:
           Birth and growth and dying
           Stem from my intention

           But of all creation
           Reared for my enjoyment
           Mortal man and woman
           Are my chosen best

Chorus   I am God the Lord
           Father, Son and Spirit
           God, the Three in One
           God whose name is Love

(*music—Theme 2*)

Son   I am God the Son
            Sight of God in action
           Into earth's existence
           I bring sense and meaning

And it is my pleasure
That all flesh should know me
So in friend and stranger
I disguise my presence

But of all emotions
In each human meeting
Love in man and woman
I regard as highest

Chorus   I am God the Lord
Father, Son and Spirit
God the Three in One
God whose name is Love

(music—Theme 3)

Spirit   I am God the Spirit
Blesser and disturber
God's own will in transit
Wandering earth invisible

And it is my pleasure
That the world should witness
How it owns its maker
And proclaim his goodness

But of all responses
To my inspiration
God is praised the clearest
Where love is incarnate

Chorus   I am God the Lord
Father, Son and Spirit
God the Three in One
God whose name is Love

(closing music)

(introductory music)

Chorus
    I am God the Lord
    Father, Son and Spirit
    God the Three in One
    God whose name is Love

(music—Theme 1)

Father
    I am God the Father
    Early in the morning
    When the world was shaping
    I made man and woman

    In the silent garden
    They walked with each other
    Naming plant and creature
    Tender nature's bounty

    But though all was perfect
    Man and woman wandered
    Far from my intention
    And from one another

Chorus
    I am God the Lord
    Father, Son and Spirit
    God the Three in One
    God whose name is Love

(music—Theme 2)

Son
    I am God the Son
    When the world most needed
    As a fellow mortal
    I met man and woman

    In the street and garden
    I spoke of forgiving
    Bringing grace and pardon
    To all human weakness

Thus can man and woman
Grow in joy and pleasure
And in love discover
Their life's true fulfilment

Chorus   I am God the Lord
Father, Son and Spirit
God the Three in One
God whose name is Love

(music—Theme 3)

Spirit   I am God the Spirit
Present to each person
Urging new creation
Thinking and conceiving

Children are my blessing
Fruit of love and waiting
Thus a human couple
Form a caring trinity

With the Son and Father
One God in communion
I surround and deepen
Holy human living

Chorus   I am God the Lord
Father, Son and Spirit
God, the Three in One
God whose name is Love

(closing music)

Making punch

Announcer: Well, now we come to our cookery spot and today Maureen Kettlewell has come along to let us into the secrets of making her special punch. Hello, Maureen.

Maureen: Hello, Richard. The basic ingredients are really pretty simple. You'll need about a dozen men, divided roughly into two groups and placed together in a large pub. Wash them down with a lot of alcohol—it doesn't really matter what, anything you've got to hand, but the important thing to get right is the quantity. Mix this all into a thick stupor and add some large slices of ego; then turn up the temperature. Just before serving, pop in a tiny little misunderstanding to give it that final zing. That should produce an excellent punch and last all evening.

Announcer: Great! Well, thanks for coming in, Maureen. That sounds devastating.

Paul Burbridge

Six short lessons in how not to have fellowship

One

Narrator: It is Sunday morning in the foyer of a church anywhere.

(Enter minister and Mrs Smith)

Minister: Good morning Mrs Smith.

Mrs S.: Good morning minister.

Minister: Lovely morning isn't it.

Mrs S.: Lovely.

Minister: How are you?

155

Mrs S.: Fine thank you. How are you?

Minister: Fine thank you. Your family well?

Mrs S.: Yes thank you.

Minister: Splendid!

Narrator: It is Sunday morning. Same place. One week later.

(Repeat exactly the same dialogue)

Narrator: It is Sunday morning. Same place. Three years later.

(Repeat exactly the same dialogue)

Narrator: How not to have fellowship Lesson One: limit the conversation to the superficial.

Two

Narrator: It is Sunday morning in the foyer of a church anywhere.

(Enter minister and a newcomer)

Minister: Ah good morning. You're a newcomer I think. Now tell me where you live. Have you been there long? You're married I see. Why isn't your husband with you? And what about children? You should bring them along too. You're a born-again Christian I hope. I think you'll find that coat of yours rather too warm in our church. I must come and look you up tomorrow. Where did you say you lived? You look as if you could afford to make a covenant, so I'll bring the forms along with me. And we're getting up a petition about abortion which I'm sure you'll want to sign. Well just go in and sit well up to the front. . . .

Narrator: How not to have fellowship Lesson Two: get personal too soon.

Three

Narrator: It is Sunday morning inside a church anywhere.

(Minister is present. Enter worshipper I)

Minister: Good morning. Nice to see you this morning. Do feel free to sit wherever you like.

(Worshipper I sits at one end of a row of chairs. Enter worshipper II)

Minister: Good morning. Nice to see you. Do feel free to sit anywhere.

(Worshipper II sits at the other end of the row of chairs.)

Narrator: How not to have fellowship Lesson Three: sit as far away as possible from anyone else in the church.

Four

Narrator: It is Sunday morning in the foyer of a church anywhere.

(A regular worshipper is welcoming a newcomer)

Reg. Wor.: Hello there! You're new here aren't you? Well, we're really pleased to see you. I'm Billy (Daisy)—though in this place I usually get called Silly Billy (Crazy Daisy). We're like that here. Just a bit of fun. Got to have a sense of humour. You'll love it here, you really will. We're a crazy lot but we do love the Lord. Hey there, Dick and Janet—come and meet our new friend here—he's dying to meet you. What did you say your name was? . . .

Narrator: How not to have fellowship Lesson Four: overdo it.

Five

Narrator: After a church service anywhere.

(One worshipper is trying to strike up a conversation with another)

A: Good morning.

B: 'morning.

A: Lovely morning isn't it?

B: Yes.

A: Keeping well?

B: Yes thanks.

A: What did you think of the service this morning?
B: All right.
A: Will you be coming to the meeting tomorrow?
B: Don't expect so.
A: Perhaps you've something else on?
B: Not really.
A: I see. Oh well. Goodbye.
B: Goodbye.
Narrator: How not to have fellowship Lesson Five: give nothing of yourself away.

Six

Narrator: After a church service anywhere.
   (One worshipper is speaking to another)
A: Hello. Haven't seen you for a while. How are you?
B: I've been in hospital for an operation.
A: Really! It's three years since I had mine. Awful it was. I got this pain, see, and I went to the doctor and I said, 'Doctor, I've got this pain,' see, so he said, 'Get on the bed,' and he prodded and poked and he said 'I think we'd better send you up for an X-ray,' so I had this X-ray and it was ages before the results came through . . .
   (and so on ad lib.)
Narrator: How not to have fellowship Lesson Six: don't let the other person get a word in edgeways.

John Horner

PART EIGHT

Appendix

Benedictions
Scripture references
Peace and war
Women in the Bible
Light
Use of recorded music
Bread
Music for meditation
Books on dance

Benedictions

Any one of these can be said, either individually or by everybody, at the close of a service.

Know ye that the Lord, he is God; it is he who hath made us, and not we ourselves; we are his people, and the sheep of his pasture. For the Lord is good; his mercy is everlasting, and his truth endureth to all generations. (Psalm 100:3, 5)

The Lord watch between me and thee, when we are absent from one another. (Genesis 31:49)

Then the peace of God, which is beyond our utmost understanding, will keep guard over your hearts and your thoughts, in Christ Jesus. (Philippians 4:7)

Peace is my parting gift to you, my own peace, such as the world cannot give. (John 14:27)

And Jesus said to his disciples, 'As the Father sent me, so I send you.' Go now in the peace of Christ into the world. 'But as for me, I keep watch for the Lord, I wait in hope for God my saviour; my God will hear me.' (Micah 7:7)

I will walk in the presence of the Lord in the land of the living. (Psalm 116:9)

This is the day on which the Lord has acted: Let us exult and rejoice in it. (Psalm 118:24)

The Lord will guard against all evil; he will guard you, body and soul. The Lord will guard your going and your coming, now and for evermore. (Psalm 121:7–8)

For in the Lord is love unfailing, and great is his power to set people free. (Psalm 130:7)

Let all praise the name of the Lord, for his name is high above all others, and his majesty above earth and heaven. (Psalm 148:13)

Let everything that has breath praise the Lord! (Psalm 150:6)

Go forth therefore and make all nations my disciples; baptize all everywhere in the name of the Father and the Son and the Holy Spirit, and teach them to observe all that I have commanded you. And be assured, I am with you always, to the end of time. (Matthew 28:19–20)

Scripture references

Peace and war

The following list of Scripture references is offered to give suggestions for readings, sermon material or meditations for worship or vigils which focus on peace and war.

Old Testament
Exodus 14:13–14. 'Moses said, "Do not fear . . . the Lord will fight for you while you keep silent."'
Exodus 15:1–19. Songs of Moses and Israel praising God's victory and strength over the Egyptians at the Red Sea.
Deuteronomy 30:15–20. 'Choose life and then you and your descendents will live . . .'
Joshua 6:1–25. The conquest of Jericho.
Joshua 10:8–15. The Lord's victory over the kings who sought to attack Gideon.
Judges 7:14–23. Gideon's trust in God and victory over Midian.

1 Samuel 8:10–22. Through Samuel the Lord warns the people against having a king.

1 Samuel 17:1–58. The story of David and Goliath.

Psalm 20:6–9. 'Some boast in chariots and some in horses, but we will remember our Lord.'

Psalm 27. 'The Lord is my light and salvation. The Lord is the defence of my life.'

Psalm 34. Encouragement to the righteous and description of what will happen to the unrighteous.

Psalm 46. 'God is our refuge and strength, a very present help in trouble ... he breaks the bow, snaps the spear ...'

Psalm 51. A plea to God, for cleansing, renewal, and sustenance.

Psalm 62. 'The Lord is my rock and salvation.'

Psalm 130. A cry to Yahweh for help and praise to Yahweh for his mercy and redemption.

Isaiah 9:6–7. 'And he shall be called the Prince of Peace ... and boundless the peace.'

Isaiah 2:2–4. 'In the last days, the Lord will be stablished chief and will judge between the nations and nations will no longer lift up swords against each other ... will beat their swords into plowshares.'

Isaiah 30:1–18. 'Woe to all those who do not follow the Lord.'

Isaiah 31. 'Woe to those who look to Egypt for help and not to God, to those who trust in fleshly strength and not to spiritual strength.'

Isaiah 60:17–18. Description of the new Jerusalem: '... peace shall be your government.'

Isaiah 61:1–3. Exaltation of the afflicted: 'The Spirit of the Lord is upon me ...'

Hosea 10:13–15. 'Because you have plowed wickedness and reaped injustice, trusting in your way and in numerous warriors and not in God, a tumult will arise and many people will be destroyed.'

Amos 1:3, 11, 13, 2:1. The Lord speaks against Israel's crimes of violence and fury.

Jonah 3. Jonah's journey to Ninevah and, 'the people turned from their wicked ways.'

Micah 4:1–4 (ref Isaiah 2:2–4). '. . . beat their swords into plowshares . . . each shall dwell under his own vine . . .'

Micah 7:7. 'But as for me, I keep watch for the Lord. I wait in hope for God my saviour: my God will hear me.'

New Testament

Matthew 5:3–11 (ref Luke 6:20–26). The Beatitudes.

Matthew 5:21–24. 'You have heard, thou shalt not kill, but I say everyone who is angry against someone is guilty and needs to seek reconciliation.'

Matthew 5:38–48 (ref Luke 6:27–36). 'Not an eye for an eye . . . but return good for evil. Love your enemies and pray for those who persecute you.'

Matthew 6:24 (ref Luke 16:13). 'No one can be slave to both God and money.'

Matthew 6:33 (ref Luke 12:31). 'Set your hearts on God's kingdom.'

Matthew 10:28 (ref Luke 12:4–5). 'Fear only the one with authority to cast into Hell.'

Matthew 16:23–26. 'Whoever loses his/her life for my sake shall save it.'

Matthew 18:21–22. Forgive seventy times seven.

Matthew 22:34–40. Two great commandments: love of God and of neighbours.

Matthew 25. The last judgement: 'Whatever you do to the least of these . . .'

Matthew 26:51–52 (ref John 18:10–11). Jesus rebukes Peter for having struck off the ear of the high priest's servant.

Luke 6:27–36. 'Love your enemies and do good to those who hate you.'

Luke 9:53–55. Jesus rebukes His disciples for suggesting fire consumption upon Samaria.

Luke 10:30–37. The Good Samaritan.

Luke 12:32. 'Do not be afraid. Your Father has chosen to give you the kingdom.'

Luke 15:11–32. The story of the prodigal son.

Luke 17:20–21. The kingdom of God is in our midst.

John 3:16–17. Eternal life in the Son.

John 11:25–26. Jesus is the resurrection and whoever believes will never die.

John 13:34–45. 'A new commandment . . . love one another . . .'

John 14:27–31. 'Peace I leave with you . . . I go away and I will come again . . .'

John 15:1–17. The vine and the branches.

John 15:18–25. 'Because you are not of this world the world hates you . . . treat you as they treated me because they do not know who sent me.'

John 16:33. 'In me you may have peace. In the world you have tribulation, but I overcame the world.'

Acts 19:23ff. Paul's preaching the gospel hurts the business of the silversmiths.

Romans 8:24–25. We must be content to hope that we shall be saved without salvation in sight.

Romans 8:36–37. In death we conquer through Him who loves us.

Romans 12. Live a transformed life.

Romans 12:9–16. 'Sincerely love each other . . . work for the Lord with great earnestness . . . keep praying when trials come.'

Romans 12:14–21. Never repay evil with evil and never try to get revenge but conquer evil with good.

Romans 13:8–14. 'Love your neighbour as yourself.'

Romans 15:2–3, 5–7. Honesty is a way of loving others.

2 Corinthians 5:15–17. Through Christ's death, we are new creatures of the spirit.

2 Corinthians 5:18–21. We are entrusted with the message of reconciliation.

2 Corinthians 10:3–6. 'For though we walk in the flesh, we do not war according to the flesh.'

Ephesians 1:15–23. 'May God reveal his wisdom to you and give you hope. He is most triumphant and supreme.'

Ephesians 2:13–18. Through Christ all people are

brought together; new peace is established by the death of the flesh, making all persons one and putting to death the enmity.

Ephesians 3:10. '. . . through the church, the wisdom of God might be made known to the rulers and authorities . . .'

Ephesians 5:1–2. Imitate God and follow Christ by loving as He loved.

Ephesians 6:10–17. 'Put on the armour of God to resist evil . . . the fight is against the powers and principalities of this dark world . . .'

Colossians 1:12–20. Thanks to God for all the wonderful things He has done.

Colossians 1:19–23, 2:13–15. Through Christ's death on the cross we are reconciled to God.

Colossians 1:27. God's purpose was to reveal His message to everyone, whether they believe or not. 'Christ's mystery is among you.'

Colossians 3:10, 12–14. Likeness to God shines forth in forgiveness and love.

Titus 2:11–14. God's grace has been revealed and we have been taught to follow Him.

Hebrews 11. 'Faith is the assurance of things hoped for, the conviction of things not seen.' Examples of faith given.

James 3:13. Wisdom is shown in meekness.

James 3:18. 'The harvest of justice is sown in peace for those who cultivate peace.'

James 4:1–5. 'What causes conflicts and quarrels among you?'

James 4:10. 'Humble yourselves before the Lord and you will be exalted.'

James 5:14–16. The church community helps those who suffer.

1 Peter 3:8–17. Love each other, keep away from evil and seek peace. 'It is better to suffer for doing right than for doing wrong.'

1 Peter 4:8–11. Use your gifts as service.

1 John 1:1–5. God is light and in Him there is no darkness.

1 John 4:7–16. 'Let us love one another, for love is from God.'

1 John 5:4. Faith overcomes the world.

from The Sojourners community

Women in the Bible

Genesis 16, 27:5–17.
Exodus 1:15–21, 15:20–21.
Joshua 2:2–22.
Judges 4:4–24, 5:6–18, 24–31.
1 Kings 21:1–16.
2 Kings 4:8–37.
Matthew 15:21–28, 25:1–13.
Luke 1:26–55, 4:38–39, 7:36–50, 8:1–3, 8:40–56, 10:38–42, 13:10–17, 13:20–21, 18:1–8, 21: 1–4, 23:27–31, 23:49, 55–56, 24:1–11.
John 4:3–42, 8:3–11, 11:20–27, 19:25, 20:1–2, 11–18.
Acts 9:36–42, 10:13–15, 40.

from No Longer Strangers

Light

Genesis 1:1–5. The creation of light.
Psalm 27:1–6. The Lord is my light and my salvation.
Psalm 30:1–5. Joy comes in the morning.
Isaiah 9:2–7. The future King.
Matthew 5:14–16. Light for the whole world.
Luke 2:29–32. A light to lighten all nations.
Luke 11:33–36. The light of the body.
John 1:1–9. The real light.
John 3:16–21. Light has come into the world.
John 8:12–19. Jesus, the light of the world.
John 12:44–50. 'I have come into the world as light.'
Ephesians 5:6–14. Live in the light.

1 Thessalonians 5:1–11. The day of the Lord's coming.
1 John 1:5–7. God is light.
Revelation 21:22–22:5. The glory of God's light.

Bread

Exodus 16:4–5, 11–12. The Lord provides food for His wandering people.
Ecclesiastes 11. Cast your bread on the water.
Luke 4:1–4. The temptations of Jesus.
Mark 6:36–44. The feeding of the five thousand.
Luke 22:14–19. The last supper.
Luke 24:30–31. Jesus is known in the breaking of bread.

Use of recorded music

Points to remember:

The use of recorded music is not an excuse for brightening up services; it is not part of a tortuous 'trying to be relevant' strategy; and it is not part of a 'they'll respect me if they think I am familiar with "their" music, i.e. "that" music' mentality.

The use of recorded music springs from incarnational theology, which states that Jesus is the Lord of all culture, and our God is the Lord of all life. Music used sensitively can create atmosphere, can broaden and widen religious and spiritual appreciation and understanding, and can make clearer Scriptural truths.

Remember also that much care and attention must be given to finding the right music and ensuring that if there are words they do not detract. Music should not stop dead; it should be quietly phased away in volume unless, of course, a dramatic effect is in mind when a sudden stop becomes suitable.

Music should be relatively short, or if long then

punctuated with words inserted at the right places, taking care not to overlap any lyrics. If you are inserting spoken material it should be brief and pointed. Remember you are not telling a story, preaching a sermon, or giving an address. You are aiding people to contemplate, meditate, and come to a richer understanding of gospel truth. Obviously you must establish a balance between your voice and the music's volume, and avoid using your voice over parts of the music where there is a pronounced heightening of volume, eg a sudden drum flurry, pounding of bass or a fiery guitar break.

Ensure that you have really good equipment: a small ineffective tape recorder or sound system should be outlawed. Ensure also that you can regulate volume and tonal shade; that you can cope with the room's and the building's acoustics; and that sound doesn't swirl, become lost or muffled.

Taped music is best, if well recorded, since it should prevent the end of an album's previous track being heard (or the beginning of the following track!) It also prevents accidents such as a sudden knocking of the record arm across the record being picked up, or even, horror of horrors, the wrong side or track being played. However, if you have taped music make sure you leave five seconds blank at the beginning of a tape before recording and also ensure you know how many seconds separate one piece from another. Ideally time everything! If you can afford it (and, why not, since cassette tapes an be re-used) use separate tapes for each piece of music. A double tape-playing machine is helpful since you can load both sides. This means that while one is playing the other can be prepared, or better still the first can be made ready after the initial tape has been played and you have passed to the second source.

There is no excuse for lack of preparation time. Always ensure things have been run through, and remember that when people are in the room everything sounds a trifle different to the way it did when the room was empty.

If at all possible operate the machinery out of the public gaze, because inevitably there will be distraction if you are seen busying yourself, and this will be made worse should things go wrong. Some churches have sound systems, so acquaint yourself with them.

The playing of music should run with close attention not only to acoustics but also to lighting. You may find the dimming of lights effective even to the point of darkness, but do things gradually. If you dim lights then learn to bring the music in line with this dimming so that as the light decreases, the sound gradually increases. Unusual light and darkness can be disturbing and even bring giggles and laughter from the more readily humoured or the perceptive who recognise the 'botch' and are not able to contain either amusement or distaste! All this means lots and lots of planning and foresight. There are no short cuts and though you may find things go a little astray at first you will soon improve and worship will be enriched.

Lastly, ensure you have given respect to the music you play and to the artist: be sensitive to the mood and do not pillage to suit your own ends. Also make sure your church and hall is registered for the playing of recorded music. The payment rate for registering is minimal.

Music for meditation

Countless records from current music can aid meditation on specific themes or scripture passages. This can be done by using instrumental passages that create a mood by using (with care and respect for the integrity of the original) appropriately vocalised sections where the lyrics aid scriptural or thematic understanding.

A number of short, sharp excerpts of specific songs can equally be played with an appropriate scripture or commentary between each song, setting biblical perspective against secular thought. To take one simple illustration: play part of Queen's 'Another One Bites The Dust'. Against the message of the song set the gospel message that the good news is for all whatever their situation.

To list useful albums is to enter a possible time-warp but there are records that retain appeal outside the normal fluctuations of charts and cult popularity. In the main, records possessing a melodic nature will be preferable to a pounding heavy metal onslaught although it depends a lot on location and the cultural ethos of those attending the service.

Albums lending themselves to the purposes outlined include:

Camel—Stationary Traveller (SKL 5334)
Supertramp—Famous Last Words (AMLK 63732)
U2—October (ILPS 9680)
U2—The Unforgettable Fire (U25)
U2—War (ILPS 9733)
U2—Under A Blood Red Sky (IMA 3)
Barclay James Harvest—Concert for the People (POLD 5062)
Simple Minds—Celebration (SPART 1183)
Todd Rundgren—Healing (AAL/BHS 3522)
Ultravox—Quartet (CDL 1394)
Working Week—Working Nights (V2343)
The Cure—Faith (FIX 6)
The Smiths—Meat Is Murder (Rough 81)
Genesis—Duke (CBR 707)
Police—Ghost In The Machine (AMLK 63730)
Dire Straits—Brothers In Arms (VERH 25)
Joy Division—Closer (FAC25)
Propaganda—Secret Wish (ZTT IQ3)
The Waterboys—This Is The Sea (ENCL5)
Gary Moore—Run For Cover (DIX16)
Pink Floyd—A Collection of Great Dance Songs (SHVL822)
Yes—Tormato (K50518)
Joan Armatrading—Show Some Emotion (AMLH68433)
New Order—Power, Corruption And Lies (FAC75)

171

Durutti Column—LC (FAC44)
Tangerine Dream—Exit (V2212)
Kate Bush—Hounds Of Love (KAB1)
Lone Justice—Lone Justice (GEF26288)
Sting—The Dream Of The Blue Turtle (DREAM1)
David Byrne—Music For The Knee Plays (EMI 064-24-03811)
Echo and the Bunnymen—Songs to Learn and Sing (Korova KODE 13)
Various—Street Sounds 14 (Street Sounds STSND 14)
Rush—Power Windows (Vertigo VERH 31)
Sammy Hagar—VOA (Geffen 26054)
Asia—Astra (Geffen 26413)
Spandau Ballet—The Singles Collection (Chrysalis SBTV1)
Grace Jones—Slave to The Rhythm (Island GRACE1)

It is not suggested that all material on these records is suitable nor that the sentiments expressed on some tracks can be squared with Christian teaching and belief. Obviously many more records could be listed and for information on 'religious' themes on general records there is an extensive listing found in the appendix of *Jesus and the Christian in a Pop Culture* by Tony Jasper (Robert Royce).

The growing standards in the Jesus Music world mean there can be an increasing use of material from this area without a sense of embarrassment when non-Christians are present. Artists such as Resurrection Band, Jerusalem, Barnabas, Garth Hewitt, Charlie Peacock, Steve Camp, Cliff Richard, Bryn Haworth, Steve Taylor, Leslie Phillips, Amy Grant, John Michael Talbot, Russ Taff, Mylon LeFevre, The Fisherfolk, and Stryper are among those who have many valid lyrical and musical offerings. Obviously the secular artists are known across the board in a mixed gathering whereas Jesus Music artists are largely known only in the Christian community.

Books on dance

Move Yourselves—Exploring the Bible in Movement, Mime and Dance, by Gordon and Ronni Lamont (Bible Society)

Steps of Faith, by Geoffrey and Judith Stevenson (Kingsway)

The Folk Arts in God's Family, by Patricia Beall (Hodders) (This is a general and praiseworthy collection of practical work relating the arts to worship. Parts of it are about dance.)

Praise Him In The Dance, by Anne Long (Hodders)

A Dancing People, by Sister Adelaide Ortefel (Center for Contemporary Celebration, PO Box 302, West Lafayette, Indiana 47906)

If you wish to receive *regular information* about *new books*, please send your name and address to:

London Bible Warehouse
PO Box 123
Basingstoke
Hants RG23 7NL

Name...

Address ....

....

....

....

I am especially interested in:
- ❏ Biographies
- ❏ Fiction
- ❏ Christian living
- ❏ Issue related books
- ❏ Academic books
- ❏ Bible study aids
- ❏ Children's books
- ❏ Music
- ❏ Other subjects

P.S. If you have ideas for new Christian Books or other products, please write to us too!